# FACE
## THE ISSUES

# FACE THE ISSUES

## Intermediate Listening and Critical Thinking Skills

**THIRD EDITION**

## CAROL NUMRICH

In Cooperation with NPR®

**Face the Issues: Intermediate Listening and Critical Thinking Skills, Third Edition**

Pearson Education, 10 Bank Street, White Plains, NY 10606

**Staff credits:** The people who made up the *Face the Issues* team,
representing editorial, production, design, and manufacturing, are
Rhea Banker, Andrea Bryant, Christine Edmonds, Nancy Flaggman,
Ann France, Gosia Jaros-White, Laura Le Dréan,
Christopher Leonowicz, Amy McCormick, and Sherry Preiss.
**Text design:** Patrice Sheridan
**Text composition:** TSI Graphics
**Text font:** 11/13 New Caledonia
**Photo Credits:** Page 1, Getty Images; Page 13, Photo Researchers, Inc.; Page 30, Photo courtesy of Chris Cobb;
Page 45, PhotoEdit, Inc.; Page 65, PhotoEdit, Inc.; Page 78, Getty Images, Inc.—Stockdisc; Page 91, Getty
Images, Inc.—Photodisc; Page 106, Rough Guides Dorling Kindersley; Page 123, Corbis Bettmann; Page 139,
Index Stock Imagery, Inc.; Page 152, Getty Images, Inc./Digital Vision; Page 164, Corbis

National Public Radio, NPR, *All Things Considered, Weekend All Things Considered,*
*Morning Edition,* and *Weekend Edition* and their logos are registered and unregistered
service marks of National Public Radio, Inc.

**Library of Congress Cataloging-in-Publication Data**

Numrich, Carol.
   Face the issues: intermediate listening and critical thinking skills / Carol Numrich; in cooperation with National Public
Radio. — 3rd ed.
      p. cm.
   **ISBN 0-13-199218-X**
   1. English language—Textbooks for foreign speakers. 2. Critical thinking—Problems, exercises, etc. 3. Current
   events—Problems, exercises, etc. 4. Listening—Problems, exercises, etc. 5. Readers—Current events. I. National
   Public Radio (U.S.) II. Title.

PE1128.N84 2007
428.2'4 — dc22

2006010860

**LONGMAN** ON THE **WEB**

**Longman.com** offers online resources for
teachers and students. Access our Companion
Websites, our online catalog, and our local
offices around the world.

Visit us at **longman.com.**

ISBN: 0-13-199218-X

Printed in the United States of America
13  17

# CONTENTS

# SCOPE AND SEQUENCE

| USAGE | PRONUNCIATION | INTERACTIVE PROCESSING ACTIVITIES |
|---|---|---|
| Restrictive Adjective Clauses | Intonation for Meaning | Design: criteria for evaluating beauty |
| Passive Voice | Intonation for Listing | Case Study: Profiles of the Homeless |
| Comparative Adjectives | Stress Shift Changes | Case Study: The Gates |
| Reported Speech | Contractions | Simulation: Reducing Crime in the Schools |
| Verbs of Perception | Compound Nouns | Values Clarification: School Lunches |
| Prefixes | Prefixes and Suffixes | Case Study: Continuing the Family Business |
| Real Conditionals | -ed Endings | Values Clarification: Scientific Inventions |
| Double Comparatives | /s/ versus /S/ | Advice: Shopping Tips |
| Idioms | Thought Groups and Stress | Design: Quality Home-Care Services |
| Wishes | Intonation for Questions | Case Studies: The Question of Divorce |
| Two-Word Verbs | Two-Word Verbs | Values Clarification: Dating |
| Hyphenated Adjectives | Dropped Syllables | Survey: Energy Solutions |

# INTRODUCTION

*Face the Issues: Intermediate Listening and Critical Thinking Skills* consists of twelve authentic radio interviews and reports from National Public Radio. The broadcasts were taken from *All Things Considered*, *Weekend All Things Considered*, *Morning Edition*, and *Weekend Edition*.

Designed for intermediate students of English as a second language, the text presents an integrated approach to developing listening comprehension and critical thinking skills. By using material produced for the native speaker, the listening selections provide content that is interesting, relevant, and educational. At the same time, they expose the nonnative speaker to unedited language, including the hesitations, redundancies, and various dialectical patterns that occur in everyday speech.

Each unit presents either a dialogue or a discussion of an issue of international appeal. The students gain an understanding of American values and culture as they develop their listening skills. Throughout each unit, students are encouraged to use the language and concepts presented in the listening material and to reevaluate their point of view.

The third edition of *Face the Issues* offers six new units based on broadcasts about compelling contemporary topics. In addition, two sections have been expanded. *Listening* now includes a *Listening for Inference* exercise, a critical skill for mastering comprehension of authentic language. *Looking at Language* now has two parts: *Usage*, which is grammar-based, and *Pronunciation*.

## SUGGESTIONS FOR USE

The exercises are designed to stimulate an interest in the material by drawing on students' previous knowledge and opinions, and by aiding comprehension through vocabulary and guided listening exercises. In a variety of discussion activities, the students finally integrate new information and concepts with previously held opinions.

### I. Anticipating the Issue

*Predicting:* In this two to three minute introduction, students are asked to read the title of the interview or report and predict the content of the unit. Some of the titles require an understanding of vocabulary or idiomatic expressions that the teacher may want to explain to the students. The ideas generated by the students could be written on the board. The teacher can present this as a brainstorming activity, encouraging students to say as many ideas as they have as quickly as they can.

Once the students have listened to the interview or report, they can then verify their predictions.

*Thinking Ahead:* Before listening to the audio, students are asked to discuss the issues to be presented in the interview or report. In groups of four or five, the students discuss their answers to general questions or react to statements that include ideas from the broadcast. The students draw on their own knowledge or experience for this exercise. It is likely that students will have different opinions, and the discussion, especially with a verbal class, could become quite lengthy. It is recommended that the teacher limit this discussion to ten or fifteen minutes, so as not to exhaust the subject prior to the listening exercises.

The teacher should also be aware that some students may be sensitive about some of the material discussed. The teacher should stress to students that there is room for all opinions, but at the same time, they should not feel compelled to talk about something that may make them feel uncomfortable.

## II. Vocabulary

In this section, three types of exercises are presented to prepare the students for vocabulary and expressions used in the listening selection.

*Vocabulary in a reading passage.* Vocabulary is presented in a reading passage that also introduces some of the ideas from the broadcast and provides some background information. The students should read through the text once for global comprehension. Then, as they reread the text, they match the vocabulary items with definitions or synonyms. The meaning of the new words may be derived from context clues, from general knowledge of the language, or from the dictionary.

*Vocabulary in sentences.* Vocabulary is presented in sentences that relate to the ideas in the listening selection. Context clues are provided in each sentence. The students should first try to guess the meaning of these words by supplying their own definition or another word that they think has a similar meaning. Although the students may not be sure of the exact meaning, they should be encouraged to guess. This will lead them to a better understanding of the new words. Once they have tried to determine the meaning of these words through context, they match the words with definitions or synonyms.

*Vocabulary in word groups.* Vocabulary items from the selection are presented as part of a word group. The focus is on the relationship between the vocabulary items and other words. A set of three words follows a given vocabulary item; in each set, two words have a similar meaning to the vocabulary item. It is suggested that students work together to discuss what they know about these words. Through these discussions, they will begin to recognize roots and prefixes and how these words relate to each other. The students should be encouraged to use their dictionaries for this exercise.

*Task Listening:* Students will now hear the listening selection for the first time. This exercise presents the students with a targeted comprehension task before asking them to focus on main ideas and details. The "task" is purposely simple; students listen for a specific piece of information in the recorded material while listening globally. Consequently, most of the students should be able to answer the questions after the first listening.

*Listening for Main Ideas:* The second time students hear the broadcast, they focus on the main ideas. Each interview or report has between three and five main ideas used to divide the selection into parts. Each part is introduced by a beep on the audio. The students are asked to choose the answers that best express the main ideas. The teacher should stop the audio at the sound of the beep to make sure the students have chosen an answer. The students may then compare their answers to see whether they agree on the main ideas. Only one listening is usually required for this exercise; however, some classes may need to listen twice in order to agree on the main ideas.

*Listening for Details:* In the third listening, the students are asked to focus on detailed information. They are first asked to read through the questions of one part. The teacher should clarify any items that the students do not understand. Then each part of the broadcast is played. The teacher should stop the audio at the sound of the beep to allow the students time to write. The students either complete missing information in sentences or answer true/false or multiple-choice questions as they listen, thus evaluating their comprehension. Finally, in pairs, they compare answers. The teacher should encourage the students to defend their answers based on their comprehension. Students should also be encouraged to use the language from the audio to convince other students of the accuracy of their answers. There will certainly be disagreements over some of the answers; the discussions will help focus attention on the information needed to answer the questions correctly. By listening to each part another time, the students generally recognize this information. Once again, they should be asked to agree on their answers. If there are still misunderstandings, the audio should be played a third time, with the teacher verifying the answers and pointing out where the information is heard on the audio.

*Listening for Inference:* The final listening activity focuses on inference. Students listen to different segments from the broadcast and are asked to infer or interpret the attitudes, feelings, points of view, or intended meanings expressed. To do this, they focus on speakers' tone of voice, stress and intonation patterns, and choice of language. Students may express slightly varied interpretations in their answers. This is to be expected, since inference can be subjective. This difference in interpretation can be a starting point to an interesting discussion. For this reason, there are *suggested answers* in the Answer Key.

## IV.    Looking at Language

*Usage:* In this exercise, a specific use of language from the listening selection is presented in isolation, as a further aid to comprehension. A wide variety of grammatical, semantic, and functional points are presented. The *Scope and Sequence* on pages vi–vii lists the usage points from the twelve units. Students are asked to listen to an example from the listening selection and to focus on this use of language in context. Then, through discussions and exercises, the students practice the language in a different context. These exercises are not meant to be exhaustive but rather to make students aware of a particular grammar point. The teacher may want to supplement this exercise with material from a grammar-based text.

*Pronunciation:* Like *Usage*, *Pronunciation* focuses on segments from the broadcast that present particular points critical to listening comprehension. Examples of intonation, stress and rhythm, and pronunciation are presented in isolation, as a further aid to comprehension. The *Scope and Sequence* on pages vi–vii lists the pronunciation points from the twelve units.

## V.    Follow-Up Activities

In this section, two activities are presented. The teacher may choose to do one or both. The students should be encouraged to incorporate in their discussions the vocabulary and concepts that were presented in the interview or report. It is expected that the students will synthesize the information gathered from the broadcast with their own opinions.

*Discussion questions:* In groups, the students discuss their answers to one or more of the questions. Students will most likely have different points of view, and should be encouraged to present their views to each other.

*Interactive processing activities:* Each activity begins with an optional listening and note-taking exercise in which the students listen again to the interview or report for important details. By listening with a particular focus, students will be better prepared to complete the interactive processing activities that follow. The *Scope and Sequence* on pages vi–vii lists the activities from the twelve units. In these activities, students must solve problems or develop ideas that recycle the language and concepts in the interviews and reports. As students complete these activities, they will have an opportunity to examine their beliefs about the issues presented. While each activity has a particular structure, there is ample opportunity for creativity and discussion.

# ACKNOWLEDGMENTS

Many people have contributed to the life of this book, both in terms of its content and the refinement of individual activities.

I am grateful to the staff at Longman for their vision and continued support for my work. Many people have been invaluable throughout the development of this text. For this third edition, I am particularly indebted to Sherry Preiss, Amy McCormick, Andrea Bryant, and Gosia Jaros-White for their helpful suggestions and skillful editing.

My colleagues at the American Language Program have been instrumental in helping me select content and develop specific exercises of this text. I would like to express particular thanks to Frances Boyd, Gail Fingado, Mary Jerome, Jane Kenefick, Linda Lane, Polly Merdinger, David Quinn, and Shelley Saltzman.

As always, I am indebted to the staff at National Public Radio for the support they continue to provide in developing materials for students of English as a second language. Special thanks go to Barbara Vierow for helping us to realize yet another edition, Wendy Blair for her continued enthusiasm for the project and superb production skills, and Frank Stasio, whose voice has become such an important part of the *Issues* series!

# Beauty Is in the
# *Mind* of the Beholder

## I. ANTICIPATING THE ISSUE

### A. PREDICTING

"Beauty is in the eye of the beholder" is a common expression. Read the title. How is it different from the expression? Discuss what you think the unit is about.

### B. THINKING AHEAD

In groups, discuss your answers to the following questions.

1. If you were a judge in a beauty contest, what would you look for? How would you evaluate someone's beauty?

2. Is the concept of beauty a cultural value? How is beauty different from culture to culture? Give examples.

3. Does one's concept of beauty change with age or circumstances? If so, how?

## II. ▶ VOCABULARY

Read the following sentences. The boldfaced words will help you understand the interview. Guess the meaning of these words from the context of the sentences. Then write a synonym or your own definition.

1.  Beauty is a question of *perception*; not everyone sees beauty in the same way.

    _____

2.  There were many attractive women who entered the beauty *pageant* in Alberta, Canada this year. The winner was from Alberta!

    _____

3.  When George proposed marriage to Eva, it only took her a *split second* to say "Yes!"

    _____

4.  Some people feel that *inner beauty* is much more important than good looks.

    _____

5.  Susan's parents and friends were *thrilled* that she had won the beauty contest.

    _____

6.  Justin's wife is quite fun and *bubbly*; she is always very entertaining.

    _____

7.  This year there were many talented *contestants* who competed in the beauty contest.

    _____

8.  I can tell that she has a lot of *confidence* by the way she walks and talks. She does not seem to be afraid of anything!

    _____

9. Julia runs all the business meetings because her partner, Joe, is too ***wimpy***. He hates making decisions and talking in front of people.

_____

10. Erin's husband is very ***outgoing***. Everyone at the party really liked him.

_____

11. Her true beauty was ***evinced*** when she said she did not want special treatment for her achievements.

_____

Match the words with their synonyms or definitions.

_____ 1. perception

_____ 2. pageant

_____ 3. split second

_____ 4. inner beauty

_____ 5. thrilled

_____ 6. bubbly

_____ 7. contestant

_____ 8. confidence

_____ 9. wimpy

_____ 10. outgoing

_____ 11. evince

a. show; clearly display

b. wanting to meet and talk to new people

c. weak and afraid

d. happy and friendly

e. contest in which people are judged on various qualities

f. person who competes in a contest

g. wonderful personality

h. belief in your ability to do things well

i. the way you understand something and your beliefs about it

j. excited and pleased

k. moment; very short period of time

# III. LISTENING

## A. TASK LISTENING

Listen to the interview.  Find the answer to the following question.

How old is Harold Grace?

## B. LISTENING FOR MAIN IDEAS

Read the questions for each part.  Listen to the interview again.  It is divided into four parts.  You will hear a beep at the end of each part.  As you listen, circle the answer that expresses the main idea in that part.  Compare your answers with those of a partner.

**Part 1**     What is unusual about Harold Grace as a beauty pageant judge?

a.  He lives in Alberta.

b.  He is blind.

c.  He is a fund-raiser.

**Part 2**     Which of these senses does Harold use to judge beauty?

a.  smell and taste

b.  taste and sound

c.  sound and touch

**Part 3**     When did Harold's sense of beauty change?

a.  when he lost his vision

b.  when he got older

c.  when he married his wife

<blockquote>**Part 4**</blockquote>   What is an important part of Harold's definition of beauty?

> a. personality
>
> b. good looks
>
> c. age

## C.  LISTENING FOR DETAILS

Read the statements for Part 1.  Then listen to Part 1 again and decide whether the statements are true or false.  As you listen, write *T* or *F* next to each statement. Compare your answers with those of a partner.  If you disagree, listen again.

<blockquote>**Part 1**</blockquote>

_____   1.  Beauty is in the eye of the beholder.

_____   2.  A beauty pageant was held in Edmonton, Alberta.

_____   3.  Harold Grace was a judge for two beauty pageants.

_____   4.  It was not easy for Harold to decide whether or not he would be a judge.

_____   5.  Harold raises funds for civic projects.

_____   6.  Harold was filled with fear about being a judge.

Repeat the same procedure for Parts 2–4.

<blockquote>**Part 2**</blockquote>

_____    7.  Harold has not done many things in his life.

_____    8.  Harold's wife has a happy and friendly personality.

_____    9.  Harold can tell whether or not a contestant is looking at him.

_____   10.  He can judge whether a person is heavy or light from the footsteps.

_____   11.  Harold likes people who have wimpy handshakes.

> **Part 3**

_____ 12. Harold lost his sight when he was fifteen years old.

_____ 13. When Harold was a teenager, he cared more about physical beauty than he does now.

_____ 14. Harold's wife had an opinion about Harold's role as a judge.

> **Part 4**

_____ 15. Harold thinks an outgoing person is beautiful.

_____ 16. He doesn't think a person should show his/her sensitivity.

_____ 17. The interviewer thinks Harold fits his own definition of beauty.

## D.  LISTENING FOR INFERENCE

Read the following statements. Then listen to the excerpts from the interview. Circle _true_ or _false_ for each statement. Compare your answers with those of a partner. Listen again if necessary.

### Excerpt 1

1. Harold had to pick his wife up off the floor when       True     False
   he told her about being a beauty pageant judge.

### Excerpt 2

2. Harold hears his wife's voice when he judges in a       True     False
   beauty pageant.

### Excerpt 3

3. Harold prefers a contestant who looks at              True     False
   him when he talks.

### Excerpt 4

4. Harold likes a firm handshake.                         True     False

**Excerpt 5**

5.  Harold's wife agreed with his pageant judging.     True     False

**Excerpt 6**

6.  The interviewer likes Harold's definition of beauty.     True     False

# IV.  LOOKING AT LANGUAGE

## A.  USAGE: Restrictive Adjective Clauses

**Notice**

Listen to the excerpt from the interview.  Focus on the underlined groups of words.  How do they function in the sentence?

Well, I think my definition of beauty is someone <u>who's reasonably outgoing, full of fun, laughter</u>.  Just someone <u>who shows caring and true sensitivity</u>.

**Explanation**

The underlined groups of words function as adjectives.  Each group begins with the relative pronoun *who*, which refers to the noun *someone*.

Restrictive adjective clauses such as those in the excerpt describe, identify, or give further information about people and things.  They are introduced with the relative pronouns *that*, *who*, *whom*, *which*, *where*, and *when*.  Look at how the following relative pronouns are used.

*who* = for people
*which* = for things
*that* = for both people or things

A beautiful person is someone **who (that)** is outgoing.
Beauty is something **which (that)** is judged by all of our senses.

*whom* = used when the relative pronoun functions as the object in the clause

That contestant is someone [**whom  Harold  admires**.]
object     subject     verb

**Exercise**

Read the following sentences.  Write the correct relative pronouns from the list below.

that    who    which    where    when    whom

1.  Harold Grace is the judge _____ lost his vision fifteen years ago.

2.  Alberta, Canada is the place _____ the beauty pageants were held.

3.  To Harold, beauty is a sound _____ is soft and bubbly.

4.  Harold prefers contestants _____ he can sense are facing him.

5.  Harold listens to the place _____ the contestant's voice is.

6.  According to Harold, a firm handshake is one _____ shows a confident person.

7.  The teenage years are a time _____ many people focus on physical beauty.

8.  Harold's wife is a woman _____ supports her husband's role as a beauty pageant judge.

9.  A beautiful person is someone _____ Harold considers to be sensitive and caring.

10. The Edmonton studios are the studios _____ the interview with Harold Grace was conducted.

## B.   PRONUNCIATION: Intonation for Meaning

**Notice**

Listen to the excerpt from the interview.  Focus on Harold's answer.  Draw a rising (—➤) or falling (—➤) arrow over his answer to show the intonation pattern.  Think about the meaning or attitude that is expressed by intonation.  Write a few words to describe what meaning or feeling you think Harold is expressing with his intonation.

LYDEN:           "You lost your sight just fifteen years ago.  How old are you?"

MR. GRACE:      "Fifty-one."

Meaning/Feeling:  _____

**Explanation**

In the excerpt, Harold uses a rising intonation pattern.  Even though his answer is a simple, factual statement, his rising intonation shows uncertainty.  This does not mean that he is uncertain of his age, but he may be unsure of what the interviewer is going to ask next.  Or, he may be wondering why the interviewer is asking him this question.

Intonation patterns can express different meanings or feelings.  A statement is usually expressed with falling intonation, but it is sometimes expressed with rising intonation, as in the excerpt.  A question is often posed with a rising intonation, but is sometimes posed with a falling intonation to express a different meaning.  Rising intonation tends to express incomplete information, a questioning position; falling intonation tends to express more complete information, a more sure position.

### Exercise 1

Work in pairs. Take turns asking the questions. Then listen to your teacher reading the answers with both a falling intonation pattern and a rising intonation pattern.

1.  How old is the contestant?
    a.  Twenty-two.
    b.  Twenty-two.

2. Would you like to be a judge, Harold?

   a. Why not?

   b. Why not?

3. What do you listen for in a candidate?

   a. Her voice direction and their footsteps.

   b. Her voice direction and their footsteps.

4. Did you hear who was chosen to judge the beauty pageant?

   a. Harold Grace, wasn't it?

   b. Harold Grace, wasn't it?

5. Who agrees with the idea that beauty is in the *mind* of the beholder?

   a. You do, don't you?

   b. You do, don't you?

6. What was Harold's wife's response to his pageant judging?

   a. She agreed with his selection, didn't she?

   b. She agreed with his selection, didn't she?

7. Which contestant seems more confident to you?

   a. The one with the firm handshake.

   b. The one with the firm handshake.

8. What is Harold's definition of beauty?

   a. Someone who is outgoing and caring.

   b. Someone who is outgoing and caring.

## Exercise 2

Work in pairs. Take turns reading the questions and answers above with both a falling intonation pattern and a rising intonation pattern. Discuss the differences in meaning.

## V. ▷ FOLLOW-UP ACTIVITIES

### A. DISCUSSION QUESTIONS

In groups, discuss your answers to the following questions.

1. Do you agree with the idea that "beauty is in the mind of the beholder?" Why or why not? Give specific examples to support your opinion.

2. It is often said that losing one sense strengthens the other senses. Imagine being a judge who has lost one of the five senses. What would you look for in judging the following contests? What would you use to judge? Write your notes in the "Comments" column.

| SENSE LOST | EVENT JUDGED | COMMENTS |
|---|---|---|
| Hearing | Music competition | |
| Smell | New perfumes | |
| Taste | Cooking contest | |
| Sight | Art show | |
| Touch | New fabrics | |

3. Harold Grace discusses some of his ideas about what is important in judging contestants. How are his ideas different from or the same as those of judges who can see the contestants? Do you think his ideas are less important than, more important than, or equally important as the ideas of a typical judge?

## B.  DESIGN: Judges' Criteria for a Beauty Pageant

### 1.  Take Notes to Prepare

By focusing on the criteria used by Harold Grace to judge beauty, you will be better able to complete the **design** activity that follows.

Listen to the interview again.  Take notes on the positive and negative traits Harold Grace mentions in judging the contestants in a beauty pageant.  Key phrases and some examples have been provided.

| Criteria | Positive Traits | Negative Traits |
|---|---|---|
| Sound | • softness of voice _____ | _____ |
|  | _____ | _____ |
|  | _____ |  |
|  | _____ |  |
| Touch | _____ | _____ |
| Personality | _____ |  |
|  | _____ |  |
|  | _____ |  |
|  | _____ |  |

### 2.  Design

Work in groups.  Develop a beauty pageant checklist.  Consider the following points:

- What criteria should judges use in evaluating beauty?

- How do you judge physical beauty?

- How do you judge inner beauty?

Present your checklist to the class.

"Beauty is in the *Mind* of the Beholder" was first broadcast on *Weekend All Things Considered*, April 9, 2000.  The interviewer is Jacki Lyden.

# 2

# A Boy's Shelter for Street People

### A. PREDICTING

Read the title and look at the photo. Discuss what you think the unit is about.

### B. THINKING AHEAD

Work in groups. Read the following statements. Do you agree with them? Does everyone in your group have the same opinion? Discuss.

1. Society must help the people who have no homes and live on the street.

2. Most people who live on the street are there because they do not want to work.

3. Most people who live on the street have mental problems.

4. You can usually tell what people are like by the way they look.

## II. VOCABULARY

The words in the first column will help you understand the interview. Try to guess their meaning. Then read each set of words. Cross out the word that does not have a similar meaning to the word in the first column. Use a dictionary if you need help. Compare your answers with those of a partner. Discuss why these words are similar.

1. **startling**          amazing                  ~~calming~~              surprising

2. **resisted**           forgot                   opposed                 fought

3. **impressionable**     affected by others       wise                    easily influenced

4. **donations**          salaries                 gifts                   contributions

5. **volunteered**        helped                   charged                 offered

6. **commitment**         job                      duty                    obligation

7. **filthy**             dirty                    unattractive            disgusting

8. **unconditionally**    without expectation      politically             freely

9. **threatening**        frightening              interesting             scary

10. **campaign**          drive                    religion                effort

## III. LISTENING

### A. TASK LISTENING

Listen to the interview. Find the answer to the following question.

Who is interviewed with Trevor?

**B.    LISTENING FOR MAIN IDEAS**

Read the questions for each part. Listen to the interview again. It is divided into four parts. You will hear a beep at the end of each part. As you listen, circle the answer that expresses the main idea in that part. Compare your answers with those of a partner.

**Part 1**    What did Trevor Ferrell do when he learned about the homeless?

a.  He asked his parents if he could live in the city.

b.  He asked the newspaper to write about the homeless.

c.  He tried to help the homeless.

**Part 2**    What did Trevor and his father learn about street life?

a.  They found out that the homeless do not want to work.

b.  They found out that living on the street is very hard.

c.  They found out that street life is not so bad.

**Part 3**    How does the community help the homeless?

a.  People bring them food in vans.

b.  The homeless stay with families.

c.  The community helps them find jobs.

**Part 4**    What has happened to Trevor because of his work with the homeless?

a.  He has more fun.

b.  His attitude has changed.

c.  He is more afraid.

## C. LISTENING FOR DETAILS

Read the questions for Part 1. Then listen to Part 1 again. As you listen, circle the best answer. Compare your answers with those of a partner. If you disagree, listen again.

### Part 1

1. When did Trevor first realize that people were living on the streets of Philadelphia?

   a. two years ago

   b. in November

   c. twelve months ago

2. How did Trevor learn about the homeless?

   a. from friends in the suburbs

   b. from his parents

   c. from a news report

3. How did Trevor's parents react when he wanted to go to the city to help someone?

   a. They were amazed.

   b. They thought it was a great idea.

   c. They were angry.

4. What did Trevor give to a man on the street?

   a. a blanket and pillow

   b. a note saying "God bless you"

   c. food

5. What happened after Trevor's story was published?

   a. The local paper donated money.

   b. People volunteered to help.

   c. Trevor wrote a book.

Repeat the same procedure for Parts 2–4.

**Part 2**

6. Which is *not* a name of one of Trevor's street friends?

   a. Chico

   b. Ralph

   c. Big Joel

7. What is *not* mentioned as a reason why people live on the street?

   a. They lost their jobs.

   b. They have mental problems.

   c. They are dirty.

8. How long did Trevor and his father stay on the street?

   a. a few minutes

   b. a few hours

   c. a few days

9. What happened when Trevor and his father tried to stay on the street?

   a. They were cold, so they went home.

   b. They were cold, but they slept in sleeping bags.

   c. They were cold because they slept on the sidewalk.

10. How did Trevor and his father feel about their night on the street?

    a. proud

    b. not proud

    c. angry

11. What does Trevor's father think about the people living on the street?

    a. He thinks they are crazy.

    b. He does not think they have such a difficult life.

    c. He does not understand how they can live there.

**Part 3**

12. Who donates food to the homeless?

    a. fast-food chains

    b. hospital coordinators

    c. the families of the homeless

13. Who pays for the food for the homeless?

    a. the homeless

    b. no one

    c. the city of Philadelphia

14. What do the homeless need most?

    a. caring

    b. clothing

    c. food

15. Why do people accept food from Trevor?

    a. He's a youngster.

    b. He can help them to get a job.

    c. He is threatening.

**Part 4**

16. How has Trevor's life changed?

    a. He is not allowed to play with his friends as much.

    b. He is not able to play with his friends as much.

    c. He does not want to play with his friends as much.

17. How does Trevor feel about the change?

    a. It is worth it.

    b. He wishes he could help more.

    c. He is grateful for his new life.

18. What has Trevor learned from his experience?

    a. People are scary.

    b. People are nice.

    c. You should treat people according to the way they look.

19. How is the money from the book *Trevor's Place* used?

    a. His mother uses it for the family.

    b. It is used for Trevor's campaign.

    c. Trevor will use it for his college education.

**D.**   **LISTENING FOR INFERENCE**

Read the following questions and statements. Then listen to the excerpts from the interview. Decide whether the statements are likely or unlikely, based on the attitudes of the speakers. Circle your answers. Compare your answers with those of a partner. Listen again if necessary.

**Excerpt 1**

Why does Trevor say, "Not that cold!"?

| | | |
|---|---|---|
| 1. He thinks his father forgot what the temperature was. | Likely | Unlikely |
| 2. He thinks his father is exaggerating. | Likely | Unlikely |
| 3. He did not think the streets were cold. | Likely | Unlikely |
| 4. He does not want to talk about the temperature. | Likely | Unlikely |

**Excerpt 2**

How does Trevor see his new life?

| | | |
|---|---|---|
| 1. He feels his parents do not let him play with his friends as much. | Likely | Unlikely |
| 2. He misses his friends. | Likely | Unlikely |
| 3. He has fun in his work with the homeless. | Likely | Unlikely |
| 4. He feels satisfied doing his work with the homeless. | Likely | Unlikely |

# IV. LOOKING AT LANGUAGE

## A. USAGE: Passive Voice

**Notice** Listen to the excerpt from the interview. Focus on the boldfaced verbs. Who do you think is responsible for the action?

The vans go in every night serving homeless people food—food that's generously **donated** by fast-food chains, and there are volunteer coordinators of the effort, individual families. There are over a hundred families in the Philadelphia area that cook on a regular basis, and food **is taken in** and **given** freely, unconditionally to people that are on the streets and obviously have a need for someone—so much more of a need for the caring that's **exchanged** than really the food, I guess.

**Explanation** Both sentences in the excerpt are in the passive voice. We use the passive voice when we want to emphasize the receiver of the action rather than the person or thing that does the action. In the excerpt, the focus is on food rather than on the person or thing that was donating it, taking it in, or giving it away.

The passive voice is formed by the verb **be + the past participle**. The person or thing that does the action is not always mentioned. When it is mentioned, it is introduced with the word **by**. In the passive, the object of an active verb becomes the subject of the passive verb:

| ACTIVE VOICE | PASSIVE VOICE |
|---|---|
| Fast-food chains generously donate food. | Food **is** generously **donated by** fast-food chains. |
| Volunteers take food in. | Food **is taken in** (**by** volunteers). |
| Volunteers give food freely. | Food **is given freely** (**by** volunteers). |

## Exercise 1

Rewrite the following sentences.  Change them from active to passive voice.  Use *by* to introduce the person or thing that does the action.  Be sure to use the same verb tense as in the original sentence.

1.  Fast-food chains donate food to the homeless.

    *Food is donated to the homeless by fast-food chains.*

2.  Volunteers give free food to the homeless.

    _____

3.  Trevor helped homeless people.

    _____

4.  A journalist interviewed Trevor.

    _____

5.  Homeless people named the shelter "Trevor's Place."

    _____

## Exercise 2

Read the news story about Trevor's work with the homeless.  Complete the story with the verbs in parentheses.  Decide whether the focus is on the person or thing that does the action (active voice) or on the person or thing that receives the action (passive voice).  Use the simple past tense.

### New Shelter for City's Homeless

Many programs have recently been developed to help the city's homeless population.  Perhaps the most interesting program is an eleven-year-old boy's campaign to help Philadelphia's homeless.

Two years ago, eleven-year-old Trevor Ferrell and his parents, Frank and Janet Ferrell, _____*put*_____ (put) an ad in a local paper asking

<sub>1</sub>

for donations to help Philadelphia's homeless.  The paper was interested in finding out what Trevor and his parents were doing.  Later that week, Trevor

_____was interviewed_____ (interview) by the paper, and his story
                    2

_____ (publish).  After the publication of that story, many
            3

people _____ (send) donations for the homeless to Trevor and
                      4

his family.  Food _____ (donate) by fast-food chains.  Many
                              5

people _____ (volunteer) to help Trevor and his family.
                    6

Someone even _____ (contribute) a van.  Volunteers
                          7

_____ (start) to give out free food to people living on the
            8

streets.

   But Trevor Ferrell's campaign did not stop there.  Last week, a

permanent shelter for the homeless _____ (open).
                                                9

Now many of Philadelphia's homeless have a warm place to shower and sleep.

Through his hard work, Trevor has become friends with many of the

homeless people.  The people know and love him.  In fact, the shelter

_____ (name) "Trevor's Place" by the people who stay there.
            10

## B.    PRONUNCIATION: Intonation for Listing

**Notice** ▷    Listen to the excerpts from the interview.  Focus on the underlined sections.
            Does the speaker use a rising ( ⟶ ) or falling ( ⟶ ) intonation
            pattern at the end of each list?  Are the patterns similar or different?  Why?

   1. It felt so good that Trevor went back <u>the next night</u>, <u>and the next</u>,
      <u>and the next</u>.

   2. <u>Donations poured in</u>; <u>people volunteered to help</u>; <u>someone contributed
      a van</u>.

   3. There's <u>Chico</u>, <u>Ralph</u>, um . . . <u>Big Joe</u> . . .

4. Well, <u>some of them lost their jobs</u>, <u>some of them, um, have mental problems</u>, <u>some of them drink</u>, . . .

5. But, uh, <u>the sidewalk's awfully hard</u>, uh, <u>you see raw sewage here and there</u>, <u>it's, it's not easy</u>.

**Explanation**    When speakers list items, they tend to use a rising intonation pattern for each item until they finish. When speakers end on a rising intonation pattern, they indicate that their list may not be complete. There may be other examples that the speaker cannot think of or does not say. This is the intonation pattern for Excerpts 3 and 4. Excerpts 1, 2, and 5 end with a falling intonation pattern. This indicates that the speaker has finished the list.

## Exercise 1

Read the questions. Listen to the answers. Draw intonation patterns for each underlined section in the lists.

1. What did Trevor do for the man living on the street?

   He <u>brought him a blanket</u>, <u>gave him a pillow</u>, and <u>told him "good night"</u>

2. Why couldn't Trevor and his dad sleep on the streets?

   <u>It was dirty</u>; <u>they felt cold</u>; <u>they had the shelter of their car to go back to</u>

3. What does their operation do?

   They have <u>vans that go in every night</u>, <u>food donated by fast-food chains</u>, <u>individual families volunteering to help out</u>

4. What reaction do they get from the street people when they give them things?

   <u>Some of them accept the food</u>; <u>some of them don't accept the food</u>; <u>some of them accept the food after they wear them down</u>

5. Why do the street people respond better to Trevor than adults?

   They see kids as <u>nonjudgmental</u>, <u>nonthreatening</u>, <u>truly wanting to</u>
   <u>help them</u>

6. Who helped Trevor to write his book about the homeless?

   <u>His father, Frank Ferrell</u>, <u>his mother, Janet Ferrell</u>, <u>and Edward</u>
   <u>Waken</u>

### Exercise 2

Work in pairs. Take turns reading the interview questions and answers above. Focus on the intonation patterns.

## V.  FOLLOW-UP ACTIVITIES

### A.  DISCUSSION QUESTIONS

In groups, discuss your answers to the following questions.

1. In your opinion, who is responsible for taking care of the homeless? Family members of the homeless? Volunteers in the community? The city? The state? Others?

2. Trevor said that his experience with the homeless had changed his life completely. Have you ever had an experience that changed your life completely? Discuss.

3. Is Trevor's story a typical one? Have people's attitudes toward the homeless changed over the years? If so, how and why?

## B.   CASE STUDIES: Profiles of the Homeless

### 1.   Take Notes to Prepare

By focusing on some of the descriptions and feelings about the homeless, you will be better able to analyze the material in the **case studies** that follow.

Listen to the interview again.  Take notes on Trevor's story.  Key phrases and some examples have been provided.

> **Street people's reactions to Trevor's kindness**
>
> • said "God bless you"
> _____
> _____
> _____
>
>
> **Trevor's feelings about the people living on the street**
>
> • he wanted to do something for them right away
> _____
> _____
> _____
>
>
> **Reasons why people live on the street**
>
> • some lost their jobs
> _____
> _____
> _____

### 2.   Case Studies

You have listened to some reasons why people live on the street.  The reasons are often much more complex than they seem.

Work in groups of three, four, or five people.  For groups of five, choose one profile each.  For smaller groups, profiles may be eliminated or people may choose more than one profile.  Prepare to give information on your profiles to the group.  As you read, fill in the chart on page 28 with information from your profiles.  Then interview the others in your group.  Use the chart to help you talk about your profiles. Complete the rest of the chart as you listen to each other's descriptions.

After you fill in the information, use the chart to analyze and discuss the homeless situation. Follow the analyzing procedure on page 29.

### PROFILE 1: Donald

Donald has a neat appearance. He looks different from the rest of the men in the shelter where he stays. His eyes are clear; his appearance is neat; but he looks frightened.

Donald is twenty-nine and represents a new type of homeless person. He is able to work but has been forced onto the streets because he lost his job and can't find an apartment he can afford to rent.

A quiet, slender man, Donald worked for six years in a photography lab. When the company was sold to new owners, they fired more than half the employees. Since then, he has been trying to find work. He fills out application after application, but he can't get a job.

Four weeks ago, Donald lost his apartment. His unemployment money ran out. He has been on the streets ever since. He is trying to get welfare money, but he needs a permanent address where he can receive necessary documents. Without the documents, he cannot get welfare.

Donald comes from a religious family. He was taught to be kind to everyone, but he can't tolerate the life of the shelter; many of the people there are drug addicts and alcoholics. He can't sleep at night because he sees people taking drugs. He feels like he's going crazy.

Donald has no wife or children. His other relatives are living in the South. He doesn't want them to know how bad things have gotten. He wants to get out of this situation. He's sure there is a better life for him somewhere.

### PROFILE 2: Florence

Florence, forty-three, a big, broad woman, wears an evening dress and a fake white fur coat. She is five months pregnant. She is not sure who the father of her baby is. She says that she'll know when the baby is born. She says she'll keep the baby if it's a girl. She has eight other children by three former husbands. Her last husband was more than eighty years old.

Florence has been homeless for three years, on and off. She spent time in Los Angeles trying to be an actress, but she was not very successful. She also spent time in a mental institution seven or eight years ago.

Florence keeps her possessions in a locker in the bus station.  She spends her nights in the subways.  She likes it in the subways because she can spend time with friends and talk about the Lord.  She says she wants to marry God.

### PROFILE 3: Sally

Sally is a forty-five-year-old woman.  She has one missing tooth and many clothes under her old dark coat, but otherwise she appears to be an ordinary, attractive woman.  She is polite and her speech is clear.  She carries a shopping bag full of books that she says she reads.  In fact, she can intelligently discuss one of the books she is carrying.  She says she identifies with some of the characters in the story.

Sally attended twelve years of school and an additional two years at a small-town community college.  She has been living on the streets for only six weeks.  She got divorced two years ago.  Her ex-husband took most of the money after their divorce.

When Sally first came to New York, she lived in cheap hotels until she had no more money.  Then she spent many nights in the waiting room of the bus station.  Finally she got a job with a food chain, but when she asked for a job transfer, she was fired.

She has two daughters: One is twenty years old, the other is twenty-two.  The twenty-two-year-old has an apartment in the city.  However, she and Sally don't get along very well, so Sally has decided to live on the street for now.  Sometimes she sleeps in the bus station, where it's warm.

Sally tries to keep herself clean.  She always carries clean clothes and a toothbrush with her.  She takes a shower in one of the city's shelters whenever she can.  She never thought she would end up in this situation.

### PROFILE 4: George

George has white hair, a high forehead, and angry eyes.  Long ago, he taught physics at one of the city's major universities.  Now he is very ill; his speech is unclear.  He tells stories that don't make sense.  He talks about "angels."

George appears to be in his early fifties.  He carries all his things in a plastic shopping bag.  His shirt is filthy.  He is often infested with lice from sleeping on the streets.

Recently, a neighborhood church donated some clothes to George. Now, he likes to go there. He likes the people and sometimes gets a free dinner. People say that when he goes to the church he sometimes thinks clearly.

George spends many of his nights on a park bench. Sometimes he sits in an all-night cafe, when he has enough money for a few cups of coffee. When he hasn't eaten in a while, the waiter in the cafe will usually give him something to eat from the kitchen.

**PROFILE 5: Jean**

Jean, thirty-nine, spends sleepless nights walking around the neighborhood where she grew up. She enters buildings and looks through garbage to see if she can find clothes. Several years ago, she and her mother lost their home; the apartment building they lived in was burned down.

Jean was born mentally disabled. Yet when she speaks, she seems to have normal intelligence. Jean's mother was an alcoholic. She died of cancer about four years ago, and Jean has been homeless ever since.

Jean is a large woman. Her dark gray hair is freshly washed. It is important for her to stay clean. She doesn't want to smell like some of the other women in the subway. Jean often goes to a day shelter where she can get a shower and a meal.

Jean finishes her wandering every morning at six o'clock in a diner where the owner sometimes gives her two dollars. She tries to pay the owner back at the beginning of the month, when she receives her Social Security disability check.

| | Age | Education | Job Experience | Present Housing Situation | Psychological Profile | Family Background |
|---|---|---|---|---|---|---|
| Donald | | | | | | |
| Florence | | | | | | |
| Sally | | | | | | |
| George | | | | | | |
| Jean | | | | | | |

### 3. Analyzing Procedure

1. Compare and contrast the information you have categorized on the chart. Can you find any similarities or differences?

2. Try to characterize the homeless population. Can you make generalizations about who these people are? Are there any characteristics that make it difficult to generalize?

3. Reevaluate your ideas or opinions about homeless people. Look at the statements on page 13 under *Thinking Ahead*. Do you have the same opinions about these statements as before? Discuss whether or not any of them have changed.

4. Analyze further. Find out more about the homeless. Where can you get more information?

**"A Boy's Shelter for Street People"** was first broadcast on *Morning Edition*, November 30, 1985. The interviewer is Lynn Neary.

# 3

# A Rainbow Effect

### A. PREDICTING

Read the title and look at the photo. Discuss what you think the unit is about.

### B. THINKING AHEAD

In groups, discuss your answers to the following questions.

1. We often think of art as something we see in a museum—a painting or a sculpture. But there are many types of nontraditional art. Can you think of examples? Has this type of art influenced you in any way?

2. How does color affect the way we see things? Describe something you saw where colors had been changed (someone's hair, a room or building, a painting in which unusual color was used for a familiar object, etc.). How did the change in color affect your perception of that person or thing?

## II. VOCABULARY

Read the following sentences.  The boldfaced words will help you understand the interview.  Guess the meaning of these words from the context of the sentences. Then write a synonym or your own definition.

1.  This building used to be a factory, but it was **converted** into an apartment house about ten years ago.

   _____

2.  As a child, I loved looking at the rainbow's **spectrum** of light that would appear in the sky after it rained.

   _____

3.  By looking at very ordinary things in new ways, artists can get **inspired** to create their works of art.

   _____

4.  Many people didn't understand the artist's **vision**, but they enjoyed the beauty of his work.

   _____

5.  Modern art sometimes tries to **subvert** the values of our daily life which many people easily accept.

   _____

6.  The famous actor, not wanting to **reveal** his identity, often wore sunglasses and a baseball cap when he went out in public.

   _____

7.  The museum exhibited beautiful works of art, but the **aesthetics** of the building and rooms were also very pleasing.

   _____

8. This novel is about the *ordeal* of a boy who was kidnapped and taken out of the country.

_____

9. The recent reports about the number of people killed in the war really *crystallized* my opposition to it.

_____

10. His home was always in *chaos*, and he constantly tried to find a quiet place where he could find some peace.

_____

11. Everyone is talking about the new *installation* outside the office building.

_____

12. Shall I try to organize this *jumble* of papers on your desk?

_____

Match the words with their synonyms or definitions.

_____ 1.  convert

_____ 2.  spectrum

_____ 3.  inspire

_____ 4.  vision

_____ 5.  subvert

_____ 6.  reveal

_____ 7.  aesthetics

_____ 8.  ordeal

_____ 9.  crystallize

_____ 10. chaos

_____ 11. installation

_____ 12. jumble

a.  try to destroy someone's or something's power or influence

b.  an artistically beautiful or pleasing appearance

c.  a situation in which everything is confused and nothing is happening in an organized way

d.  idea of what you think something should be like

e.  something that has been put in place for use

f.  a messy mixture of things

g.  show something that was previously hidden

h.  the set of different colors that is produced when light passes through a prism

i.  make someone have a particular feeling

j.  a very bad experience that continues for a long time

k.  change from one form, system, or purpose to another

l.  become clear in one's mind

# III. ⟩ LISTENING

## A. TASK LISTENING

Listen to the interview.  Find the answer to the following question.

What does Chris Cobb call the two kinds of people who helped him?

## B. LISTENING FOR MAIN IDEAS

Read the questions for each part.  Listen to the interview again.  It is divided into four parts.  You will hear a beep at the end of each part.  As you listen, circle the answer that expresses the main idea in that part.  Compare your answers with those of a partner.

**Part 1**   What did Chris Cobb do to the Adobe Bookshop?

    a.  He converted it into a used bookstore.

    b.  He rearranged the bookshelves by color.

    c.  He turned it into a studio for artists.

**Part 2**   Why did Chris do this work?

    a.  He wanted to change something in order to see something new.

    b.  He wanted to confuse people.

    c.  He wanted to have fun at work.

**Part 3**   What discovery did Chris make about color?

    a.  There were more colors than he realized.

    b.  Not all colors fit easily into the spectrum.

    c.  Hot pink is a very popular color.

| Part 4 | How does Chris describe his team of workers? |

    a. They were not willing to take breaks.

    b. They did not like the managers.

    c. They represented two kinds of people in the world.

## C. LISTENING FOR DETAILS

Read the statements for Part 1. Then listen to Part 1 again and decide whether the statements are true or false. As you listen, write *T* or *F* next to each statement. Compare your answers with those of a partner. If you disagree, listen again.

| Part 1 |

_____ 1. The Adobe Bookshop is located in San Francisco.

_____ 2. There are exactly 20,000 books that have been arranged.

_____ 3. The color arrangement represents the spectrum.

_____ 4. Chris Cobb has dreamed of this project for thirty-four years.

_____ 5. Chris created the light in the room.

_____ 6. The color spectrum changes as you walk down the aisle.

Repeat the same procedure for Parts 2–4.

| Part 2 |

_____ 7. Chris usually works with one kind of media.

_____ 8. Chris likes to subvert the system of the media he works with.

_____ 9. With this new arrangement, people are getting confused looking for a book.

_____ 10. People are having more fun looking for used books.

### Part 3

_____ 11. The bookstore looks like a rainbow.

_____ 12. There were more hot pink books than Chris had expected there to be.

_____ 13. Hot pink fits into the normal color spectrum quite easily.

_____ 14. Hot pink was placed in between brown and white.

### Part 4

_____ 15. Chris had a dedicated group of about fifty to sixty people working with him.

_____ 16. They finished the job at 10:00 at night.

_____ 17. The stacks of books were about 3 or 4 feet high.

_____ 18. The job took ten hours.

_____ 19. Everybody was fatigued (tired of the work) at about 4:30 P.M.

_____ 20. Chris put music on to help everyone relax.

_____ 21. The project was crystallized for Chris when everyone was stressed.

_____ 22. The stackers and spreaders were a perfect combination in this project.

_____ 23. The books were set to be a multicolored jumble on December 10.

## D.    LISTENING FOR INFERENCE

Read the following statements. Then listen to the excerpts from the interview. Listen to Chris's tone of voice and word choice. What is the strongest feeling he had at each of the excerpted stages of the project? Complete the statements. Compare your answers with those of a partner. Listen again if necessary.

**Excerpt 1**

1. Chris Cobb feels _____.

   a. frustrated

   b. delighted

   c. accepting

**Excerpt 2**

2. Chris Cobb feels _____.

   a. frustrated

   b. delighted

   c. accepting

**Excerpt 3**

3. Chris Cobb feels _____.

   a. frustrated

   b. delighted

   c. accepting

# IV. LOOKING AT LANGUAGE

## A. USAGE: Comparative Adjectives

**Notice**  Listen to the excerpt from the interview. Which part of the statement is grammatically incorrect?

> Actually, what's happened is people have been saying it's something really magical and they would never see it anywhere, and it makes the process of looking for used books a lot funner.

**Explanation**  In English, most one-syllable adjectives generally add -er to form the comparative. In the excerpt, the correct form is "makes the process of looking for used books more fun." *Fun* does not follow the normal one-syllable adjective rule because it comes from a noun. However, *funner* is a common error.

Here are some general rules for forming comparative adjectives:

1.  For most short (one-syllable) adjectives, add -*er* to form the comparative. Use *than* before the person or thing you are comparing. When a one-syllable adjective ends in a consonant, double the last consonant and add -*er*.

    The books on those shelves are **older than** the ones in the box.

    The magic was **bigger** than the confusion in the bookstore.

2.  For most long (two- or more-syllable) adjectives, add *more* or *less* before the adjective.

    Stackers are **more organized than** spreaders.

    Spreaders are **less organized than** stackers.

    An exception is two-syllable adjectives that end in -*y*. Change the -*y* to *i* and add -*er*.

    The rearranged bookshelves were **prettier** than the normal multicolored jumble.

3.  Some comparative forms are irregular. The comparative of *good* is *better*. The comparative of *bad* is *worse*. The comparative of *far* is *farther/further*.

    The daytime light is **better than** the nighttime light.

    The fatigue at 4:30 in the morning was **worse than** the fatigue at 10:00 at night.

    Brown is **further** away **than** blue on the spectrum.

## Exercise

Read the following sentences. Write the correct comparative forms of the adjectives in parentheses.

1.  After Chris Cobb rearranged the used books on the bookshelves, the Adobe

    Bookstore was _____ (colorful) than before.

2.  The spectrum is _____ (red) at the beginning than it is at

    the end.

3.  After seeing the Adobe Bookshop, a customer will find a regular bookstore a lot

    _____ (interesting).

4. The natural light in the bookstore is _____ (bright) in the daytime than it is at night.

5. Looking for used books was _____ (amusing) than after they had been rearranged by color.

6. It was _____ (hard) to fit hot pink into the spectrum than it was to fit red and blue.

7. Hot pink is _____ (blue) than lavender.

8. The workers were _____ (happy) at the beginning of the project than they were in the early morning hours.

9. The workers were _____ (fatigued) after they took a break and went out for air.

10. The color red is _____ (far) from the color blue than is the color green.

11. The music was _____ (loud) during the early hours than it was later on that night.

12. The situation was _____ (ugly) at 4:30 in the morning than it had been earlier in the evening.

## B. PRONUNCIATION: Stress Shift Changes

**Notice** Listen to the excerpts from the interview. Focus on the underlined words. Mark the stressed syllable in these words with a stress mark (´).

1. The Adobe Bookshop in San Francisco has been <u>converted</u> into a rainbow of books.

2. And nobody's getting confused looking for a book maybe by, oh, <u>subject</u> or title or author or something?

3. There were books everywhere and people were getting tired and knocking over giant stacks of books and getting <u>upset</u>.

**Explanation**     English words sometimes have different syllable stress depending on their function. In Excerpt 2 above, we see that nouns usually receive stress on the first syllable. In Excerpt 1, we see that verbs usually receive stress on the second syllable. Adjectives receive stress on either the first or second syllables. In Excerpt 3, the stress is on the second.

| NOUN | VERB | ADJECTIVE |
|------|------|-----------|
| ´convert | con´ vert | — |
| ´subject | sub´ ject | — |
| ´upset | up´ set | up´ set |

## Exercise 1

Complete each pair of sentences with the correct word. Decide how the word functions in each sentence. Mark the stressed syllable.

| content | increase | object | permit | project |
|---------|----------|--------|--------|---------|
| contrast | insert | perfect | present | record |

1. Chris could not decide where to _____ the hot pink books into his color spectrum.

   The magazine had an _____ that advertised the Adobe Bookshop's exhibit.

2. Chris had to get a _____ from the Adobe Bookshop to install his exhibit.

   Chris was surprised that the bookstore owner would _____ him to rearrange all his used books into a color spectrum.

3. The _____ of Chris's experiment was to reveal something you would never see otherwise.

   The reporter thought people might _____ to looking for books that were not arranged according to subject, title, or author.

4. As books were rearranged on the shelves, you could see the colors of the book covers _____ more easily.

   The rearranged bookshelves were quite a _____ to the normal multicolored jumble.

5. Chris could not find a _____ way to fit hot pink books into the spectrum.

   Once he realized he could combine them with the lavender books, he could _____ his rainbow effect.

6. Surprisingly, _____ numbers of customers came to shop in the bookstore after Chris had rearranged the books by color.

   Once the books were rearranged by color, it was impossible to _____ them by subject or title.

7. The rainbow of books will _____ a different way of looking for books to the Adobe Bookshop customers.

   The bookstore is a nice place to shop for a _____.

8. With this installation, none of the _____ of the books changed, only the perception of the book covers.

   Chris was very _____ with the visual result of his project.

9. Did the sales of books _____ during the installation?

   There was an _____ in the number of people who came

   into the bookshop during that time.

10. The rainbow of books was a _____ that Chris had dreamed

    of doing for a long time.

    The bookstore didn't _____ that their sales would be

    affected.

### Exercise 2

Work in pairs.  Take turns reading the above sentences.  Focus on the stressed syllables.

## V. FOLLOW-UP ACTIVITIES

### A.  DISCUSSION QUESTIONS

In groups, discuss your answers to the following questions.

1. At the end of the interview, Chris Cobb says he feels that there are two kinds of people in the world: stackers and spreaders.  What does he mean?  Which type are you?  How would you work in a high-stress situation?

2. Do you agree with Chris Cobb that changing a system a little bit can "reveal something . . . that you would never see otherwise"?  Discuss another example of this.

3. How do you think you would react to the Adobe Bookshop?  Would you think it was interesting?  Would it bother you if you could not find a book easily?

## B.   CASE STUDY: The Gates

### 1.   Take Notes to Prepare

By focusing on some of the details of the artwork that was installed in the Adobe Bookshop, you will be better able to discuss the pros and cons of the art installation proposed for New York City in the **case study** that follows.

Listen to the interview again.  Take notes on the rearranging of the Adobe Bookshop in San Francisco.  Key phrases and some examples have been provided.

Where the installation was done

• Adobe Bookshop in San Francisco
_____

_____

Physical change that was made to a public space

_____

_____

Visual effect of the change

_____

_____

Vision / inspiration for the project

_____

_____

Public's reaction

_____

_____

Problems encountered in creative work

_____

_____

Reactions of workers on the project

_____

_____

When the installation will be dismounted

_____

_____

### 2. Case Study

You have listened to Chris Cobb describe his rearrangement of the books in San Francisco's Adobe Bookshop by color. Now you will read about The Gates, an art installation that was presented in New York City in 2005.

Work in groups. Imagine that you were members of the Central Park Conservancy in New York City. Read the case. Discuss whether or not you would support the project. Try to reach an agreement. Take notes on your group's discussion. You can use the chart on page 29 as a model for organizing your notes. Then present your group's decision to the class.

Christo and his wife, Jeanne-Claude, are internationally-known artists. They have created huge visual effects around the world. Some of the more famous are the wrapping of the Reichstag monument in Germany, the wrapping of the Pont Neuf in France, and the installation of blue and yellow umbrellas in Japan and California. In 1981 they proposed installing a series of gates throughout Central Park in New York City. The Parks Department turned down the project, however, feeling that the project would damage the park and bring more projects like it to the park. New York's mayor at that time also opposed the idea. He thought the Gates project was coming to "the wrong place at the wrong time." New York was going through an economic crisis in the early 1980s, and it seemed a waste of money to support such an expensive and unnecessary project.

Decades later, Christo and Jeanne-Claude have come back to propose their Gates project once again. They would like to install 7,500 gates of orange-colored cloth along 23 miles of paths in Central Park. This is half the number of gates they had proposed years ago. The installation will remain for two weeks, and then it will be torn down. The artists say that they will finance all expenses. In addition, they will pay the city $3 million to fund programs in Central Park and other parks if they are given permission to install their work.

The artists claim that "The Gates" will be a grand, spectacular, and wonderful project. They feel that it will be a symbol of joy and beauty, a ceremonial invitation to walk through the park. Even after the installation is gone, it will have left a mark on Central Park and the people who saw it, they say. Supporters of the project say that such an installation could provide a sense of humor to New Yorkers' emotional health. In fact, this positive image could replace the negative image of the collapsing World Trade Center, which so many New Yorkers continue to carry around with them. Even the current mayor supports the idea because he feels such a work of art could contribute to New York City's imaginative spirit. Moreover, it could bring a lot of money to the city, as it is expected that 500,000 tourists would visit.

In contrast, many residents of New York City are not supportive of this idea. They feel a big installation to Central Park would destroy the peace and quiet they enjoy in the park. Many people go to Central Park every day to escape the stress of the city and are not happy about 500,000 tourists invading their park. Many people say that the park is art and that they do not need more art! The original designers of Central Park, Vaux and Olmstead, saw the park as a place of beauty and quiet. An installation that requires 5,000 tons of steel would only cause destruction to this beautiful and natural environment. Finally, many believe that even though Christo and Jeanne-Claude have promised to pay for their installation and contribute money to New York City's park system, there will, in reality, be some cost to the park.

**"A Rainbow Effect" was first broadcast on *All Things Considered*, November 22, 2004. The interviewer is Melissa Block.**

# 4

# Attached to Crime

## I. ANTICIPATING THE ISSUE

### A. PREDICTING

Read the title and look at the photo. Discuss what you think the unit is about.

### B. THINKING AHEAD

In groups, discuss your answers to the following questions.

1. Are today's teenagers different from teenagers of years ago? If so, how are they different? Why are they different?

2. Describe the atmosphere in schools in your country. What kinds of problems are there in the schools? Is crime a problem?

## II. VOCABULARY

The words in the first column will help you understand the report. Try to guess their meaning. Then read each set of words. Cross out the word that does not have a similar meaning to the word in the first column. Use a dictionary if you need help. Compare your answers with those of a partner. Discuss why these words are similar.

| | | | |
|---|---|---|---|
| 1. **menace** | nuisance | threat | ~~violence~~ |
| 2. **diverse** | dangerous | different | mixed |
| 3. **committed** | determined | devoted | distracted |
| 4. **conflict** | idea | fight | quarrel |
| 5. **mediators** | teachers | negotiators | peacemakers |
| 6. **defuse** | calm | reduce tension in | concentrate on |
| 7. **chilling** | frightening | upsetting | delightful |
| 8. **humongous** | big | beautiful | huge |
| 9. **resent** | feel angry | feel afraid | feel bitter |
| 10. **banned** | restricted | prohibited | advertised |
| 11. **stiffer** | calmer | stronger | more severe |
| 12. **defiant** | supportive | fearless | bold |

## III. LISTENING

### A. TASK LISTENING

Listen to the report. Circle the best answer to the following question.

Who is most responsible for solving disputes among students in this school?

a.  the police     b.  the high school principal     c.  the students

## B.  LISTENING FOR MAIN IDEAS

Read the questions for each part.  Listen to the report again.  It is divided into six parts.
You will hear a beep at the end of each part.  As you listen, circle the answer that
expresses the main idea in that part.  Compare your answers with those of a partner.

**Part 1**    What have many American communities been unable to escape?

   a.  children taking weapons to school

   b.  children becoming menaces

   c.  children escaping their communities

**Part 2**    What has affected all the children in this report?

   a.  living in a new suburban area

   b.  living with crime

   c.  living with families who don't understand them

**Part 3**    Why have these teens begun to accept crime as a fact of life?

   a.  Racial conflicts on the news influence them.

   b.  They realize that all kids are aggressive today.

   c.  They experience it all around them.

**Part 4**    Why is the Wakefield school less violent now?

   a.  Security measures have been taken.

   b.  Beepers are used to warn people of violence.

   c.  Students protect themselves with weapons.

> **Part 5**     Why are gangs formed?

    a.  Kids are afraid.

    b.  Kids are asked by older kids to join them.

    c.  Kids decide to run away from home.

> **Part 6**     How does Koon deal with the crime problem?

    a.  with defiance

    b.  with worry

    c.  with suspicion

## C.   LISTENING FOR DETAILS

Read the questions for Part 1.  Then listen to Part 1 again.  As you listen, circle the best answer.  Compare your answers with those of a partner.  If you disagree, listen again.

> **Part 1**

1.  What are kids packing to take to school?

    a.  lunch boxes

    b.  weapons

    c.  books to read

2.  Which magazine or newspaper is *not* mentioned in the introduction?

    a.  *The Washington Post*

    b.  *Time*

    c.  *Newsweek*

Repeat the same procedure for Parts 2–6.

**Part 2**

3. How can Arlington's Wakefield High School be described?

   a. a typical American public school

   b. an ethnically diverse school

   c. small and attractive

4. Which is *not* a racial percentage of the student body?

   a. 36 percent Hispanic

   b. 50 percent Asian

   c. 24 percent black

5. How would the students describe themselves?

   a. working class

   b. poor

   c. wealthy

6. What is true about the kids in this report?

   a. They are often in conflict with other students.

   b. They are committed to solving the problem.

   c. They often feel out of control.

7. Which problem is mentioned as an example of crime that has affected the students' lives?

   a. One student's little brother sells drugs.

   b. One student has been shot.

   c. One student's family knows someone who committed murder.

8. What other incidents of crime have these students been exposed to?

   a. One student was involved in a drive-by.

   b. One student was raped.

   c. One student's mother was robbed.

#### Part 3

9. How would these kids describe the crime they see?

   a. chilling

   b. racial

   c. normal

10. Which weapon is *not* mentioned as one that is used at parties?

    a. a knife

    b. a gun

    c. a club

11. What happens when someone pulls out a gun?

    a. Someone usually gets hurt.

    b. Everybody runs.

    c. Everybody fights.

#### Part 4

12. How do the kids feel about the security measures that have been used in their school?

    a. They resent some of them.

    b. They would like more metal detectors.

    c. They want more items banned.

13. What is true about Kassen?

    a. He is eighteen years old.

    b. He has attacked other guys in the bathroom.

    c. He does not carry weapons.

**Part 5**

14. Why do kids join gangs?

    a. They cannot protect themselves.

    b. They are afraid of the kids in the gang they join.

    c. They like the name of the gang.

15. What do you have to do to be in a gang?

    a. develop rules

    b. follow rules

    c. adopt the rules of the Boy Scouts

16. Which solutions to the crime problem do the kids suggest?

    a. more parental punishment

    b. fewer gangs

    c. more serious penalties

17. Why do these kids feel attached to crime?

    a. They like it.

    b. They cannot run away from it.

    c. They want to join the criminals.

18. What does Kassen sometimes think about?

    a. moving to another country

    b. joining a gang

    c. getting killed

**Part 6**

19. Why do the kids feel defiant toward crime?

    a. They do not live in the worst neighborhoods.

    b. They cannot get away from crime.

    c. They feel safe in their houses.

20. What could be heard at the end of this report?

    a. kids with walkie-talkies

    b. security guards with walkie-talkies

    c. suspicious-looking kids in a fight

## D.   LISTENING FOR INFERENCE

Read the following statements. Then listen to the excerpt from the report. What does the speaker mean? Check (✓) all the possible interpretations. Compare your answers with those of a partner. Listen again if necessary.

_____  1. She cannot change the crime situation.

_____  2. She is a criminal, too.

_____  3. Crime is comfortable.

_____  4. She sees crime as a part of her life.

_____  5. She feels powerless in the face of crime.

_____  6. She enjoys crime.

_____  7. She never thinks about crime.

# IV.   LOOKING AT LANGUAGE

## A.   USAGE: Reported Speech

**Notice**   Listen to the excerpt from the report. Underline the three newspaper headlines that are mentioned.

> Only a few years ago, schoolchildren packed lunch boxes, and now more and more of them are packing weapons. We read about it every day. "Crisis of violence, a menace to childhood," says the *Washington Post.* "Violence hits one in four students," reports the *New York Times,* and *Newsweek* declares that "Our children are growing up scared." Surely some communities have escaped the trend, but too many have not. NPR's Lynn Neary visited a high school in Virginia and has this report.

The excerpt quotes the headlines directly from newspapers and a magazine. Words are often deleted in headlines. Here are the headlines written as full sentences in reported speech:

*The Washington Post* said that a crisis of violence is a menace to childhood.

*The New York Times* reported that violence had hit one in four students.

*Newsweek* declared that our children were growing up scared.

**Explanation**

Reported speech reports what a speaker said without using the exact words. The reporting verbs (e.g., *said, reported,* and *declared*) are usually in the simple past tense. The verbs following the reporting verbs are usually in a past form.

When quoted speech changes to reported speech, the verb tenses in the reported speech often change. In addition, pronouns change to keep the speaker's original meaning.

| QUOTED SPEECH | REPORTED SPEECH |
|---|---|
| **Present tense** | **Past tense** |
| The reporter explained, "They have been trained as mediators who can step into a dispute and help defuse it before it **gets** out of control." | The reporter explained that they had been trained as mediators who could step into a dispute and help defuse it before it **got** out of control. |
| **Past tense** | **Past perfect** |
| The reporter said, "The school principal **asked** us to use only first names, and we **agreed**." | The reporter said that the school principal **had asked** them to use only first names and that they **had agreed.** |
| **Present perfect** | **Past perfect** |
| The reporter explained, "They **have been trained** as mediators who can step into a dispute and help defuse it before it gets out of control." | The reporter explained that they **had been trained** as mediators who could step into a dispute and help defuse it before it got out of control. |
| **Present modals** | **Past modals** |
| The reporter explained, "They have been trained as mediators who **can** step into a dispute and help defuse it before it gets out of control." | The reporter explained that they had been trained as mediators who **could** step into a dispute and help defuse it before it got out of control. |
| **Pronouns** | |
| The reporter said, "The school principal asked **us** to use only first names, and **we** agreed." | The reporter said that the school principal had asked **them** to use only first names and that **they** had agreed. |

**Exercise**

Rewrite the following statements.  Change them from quoted to reported speech.
Change tenses and pronouns as needed.

1.  "In my neighborhood, it's becoming like that."

    A male student added that in his neighorhood it was becoming like that.

    _____

    _____.

2.  "My family knows two people that have had sons or daughters murdered."

    A male student admitted that _____

    _____

    _____.

3.  "There was somebody raped right at the corner of my street."

    A male student reported that _____

    _____

    _____.

4.  "Now that we've grown up with it . . . you get attached to it."

    A female student suggested that _____

    _____

    _____.

5. "I know that I'm gonna die some way, somehow, so I don't worry about it."

   A male student declared that _____

   _____

   _____.

6. "I just don't think that . . . crimes or whatever, will come to me because . . . I just

   feel like it's not gonna happen to me."

   A female student said that _____

   _____

   _____.

## B. PRONUNCIATION: Contractions

**Notice**   Listen to the excerpts from the report.  How do the speakers pronounce the boldfaced words?  How would the pronunciation change if the contracted forms were full forms?

1. I mean, **they're** just—**they're** either, like, you know, **they're** drunk or **they're**, you know, just, I mean, **they're** just not thinking, so I mean, I almost, you know, I sort of expect it to happen.

2. **We're** attached to crime.

3. It's really interesting to hear what **you're** saying because **you're** saying, "It doesn't affect me, but—"

4. I don't let it affect me because if I let—if I keep sitting home and worry about it, then **I'll** probably sit home the whole rest of my life and not go out of my house.

**Explanation**   When we use contracted forms of speech, the pronunciation of words changes.

When *are* is contracted to *'re,* the pronouns before the verb are reduced.  In Excerpts 1, 2, and 3, *they're* is pronounced like "there;" *we're* is pronounced like "were;" *you're* is pronounced like "yer."

When *will* is contracted to *'ll*, pronouns ending in [y], like *I*, or [w], like *you*, are reduced.  In Excerpt 4, *I'll* is pronounced like "ull."

Note the pronunciation of other prounouns with *'ll*: *he'll, she'll,* and *we'll* are pronounced "hull," "shull," and "wull."  *You'll* is pronounced "yull," and *they'll* is pronounced "thull."

### Exercise 1

Imagine that the students from Wakefield High School are being interviewed.  Match the questions in the left column with the answers in the right column for Groups A and B.

### Group A

| Questions | Answers |
|---|---|
| _____ 1. Why do you worry about your little brother? | a. We're nervous because she got robbed once. |
| _____ 2. Why do you feel uncomfortable when you see guys on the streets of your neighborhood? | b. Almost always, you'll see some kind of fight start. |
| _____ 3. Why is your family against your walking outside? | c. They're afraid I'll be raped. It happened to a girl a few weeks ago. |
| _____ 4. Why do you and your mom feel unsafe in Green Valley? | d. I'm afraid he'll get on drugs. |
| _____ 5. What happens if I go to a party in your neighborhood? | e. Because they're walking around with knives. |

## Group B

| Questions | Answers |
|---|---|
| _____ 1. Why will a guy pull a knife or gun at a party? | a. I guess I don't think I'll be affected by it. |
| _____ 2. What happens if kids try to take a beeper to school? | b. You know, he'll be drunk or something. |
| _____ 3. Why will kids join gangs? | c. We don't think about it because we're attached to crime. |
| _____ 4. How do you and your friends feel about the crime in your neighborhood? | d. They're afraid, so they'll seek safety in numbers. |
| _____ 5. Why don't you worry about crime? | e. They'll have it taken away because it's a banned item in our school. |

## Exercise 2

Work in pairs. Take turns reading the questions and answers above. Be sure to pronounce the contracted forms correctly. Change roles after Group A.

# V. FOLLOW-UP ACTIVITIES

## A. DISCUSSION QUESTIONS

In groups, discuss your answers to the following questions.

1. What is the best way for schools to maintain safety? Some possibilities include the use of metal detectors and uniformed police officers, and more involvement from the principal, parents, and student mediators. Can you think of other methods that could work? Explain.

2. One student in the interview said that she feels "attached to crime." Is it possible to feel attached to something terrible because you do not know how to get away from it? Give examples.

3. Imagine that you are one of the students at Wakefield High School. Describe your day. Tell what happened in school. How did you feel about it? What would you like to happen?

## B.   SIMULATION:  Reducing Crime in the Schools

### 1.  Take Notes to Prepare

By focusing on the experiences of Wakefield High School students, you will be better able to prepare for the **simulation** that follows.

Listen to the report again.  Take notes on the issues relating to crime.  Key phrases and some examples have been provided.

Examples of crime

• weapons taken to school _____

_____

_____

_____

_____

_____

_____

_____

_____

Teenagers' feelings about crime

• calm acceptance _____

_____

_____

_____

_____

_____

_____

Attempts to deal with the crime issue

• conflict-resolution programs

_____

_____

_____

_____

_____

_____

_____

_____

_____

✓ **2. Simulation**

In the report, you heard about the crime teenagers live with every day in one American city. You also heard about the teenagers' feelings about this crime and different ways to deal with crime.

To begin, follow these steps:

1. Divide the class into four groups: teachers, parents, community leaders, and the school board.

2. Read the situation.

3. Choose roles.

4. Prepare for fifteen minutes.

5. Begin the open school board meeting.

**The Situation**

Arlington's Wakefield High School has just received a $150,000 grant from the federal government to develop a program to reduce the crime problem in the school and its surrounding neighborhoods.

Teachers, parents, and community leaders have all made proposals to the school, suggesting how this money should be spent to deal with the crime problem. The school board has reviewed the proposals and will decide how the money should be spent. Before its decision, it will hold an open school board meeting for all concerned to express their opinions. After the meeting, the school board will decide which proposals will be accepted and how much money to allocate to them.

## Proposals

1. Conflict-resolution program

*Rationale:*
If students are encouraged to take responsibility for situations and work to solve the problems that lead to crime, they will be less likely to engage in crime themselves.

*Recommendations:*
Require all students to spend two hours a week in conflict-resolution and mediation classes. These courses will teach students how to defuse problems before they become bigger. The students will learn how to intervene when they see others fighting.

2. Hiring of additional social workers

*Rationale:*
More intervention is needed. Trained social workers should be assigned to work with the students and the families of students who have been involved in crime.

*Recommendations:*
Hire full-time social workers to work in the schools. They will meet weekly with students who have been involved in crimes or whose families have been involved in crimes. Part-time social workers will visit the families' homes.

3. Increasing security measures

*Rationale:*
Students will be less likely to bring weapons to school if stronger security measures are taken. There needs to be more supervision at school.

*Recommendations:*
Introduce more metal detectors at all school entrances. Hire more guards and police officers to patrol the school and its neighborhood.

4. After-school sports programs

*Rationale:*
If students have more opportunities to be occupied in after-school activities such as sports, they will be less likely to hang out on the streets and become involved with crime.

*Recommendations:*
More money should be spent on after-school sports activities. Although controversial, one program in particular, "Midnight Basketball," has been shown to be particularly effective in urban areas. Instead of spending the night on the streets, kids are invited to come into the school to play basketball late at night.

5. Parental involvement incentives

*Rationale:*
One of the reasons young people are involved in crime is because their parents are not involved in their lives. If parents were more involved in the school and their children's education, teens would be less involved in crime.

*Recommendations:*
Set up after-school activities for parents and their children, such as fairs, sports, and discussion groups. Encourage parents to volunteer at the school once a month as a "parent-teacher" to be involved in his or her child's classroom as a teacher's aide. Parents who volunteer their time will be given free training courses in local businesses. These courses could help them get higher salaries or find better jobs.

6. Consciousness-raising assemblies

*Rationale:*
Bringing teachers and students together to discuss the crime problem in an open forum can help raise the students' consciousness about the consequences of crime.

*Recommendations:*
Offer an honorarium to people (city police officers, reformed criminals, people who have lost a family member to crime) to come to the school to talk about the consequences of crime. Pay teachers overtime salaries to organize and participate in these assemblies.

7.  In-service teacher training

*Rationale:*
Studies have shown that improved classroom instruction has a direct relationship to getting students more involved with their studies and less involved with crime.

*Recommendations:*
Hire consultants to work with teachers on a long-term basis.  Bring in experts who can train teachers to redesign their lessons with an emphasis on improved teaching strategies and student-centered learning.

**The Roles**

Teachers
You teach in Wakefield High School.  You are concerned about the quality of education of your students and the safety of the school.  Review the proposals to decide which of them would help most to reduce the crime problem at Wakefield High School.

Parents
Your children attend Wakefield High School.  You are concerned about the fact that weapons have been brought to their school.  You are afraid for your children's lives.  Review the proposals to decide which of them would help most to reduce the crime problem at Wakefield High School.

Community Leaders
You are a group of religious leaders, businesspeople, and concerned citizens who live in the Wakefield High School neighborhood.  If teenagers at Wakefield High School are involved in crime, it directly affects you: the safety of the streets, business establishments, and public places.  Review the proposals to decide which of them would help most to reduce the crime problem at Wakefield High School.

School Board
You are a group of elected or appointed community leaders who set school policy.  You have reviewed all proposals for reducing the crime problem at Wakefield High School and its surrounding neighborhood.  You are interested in hearing the various opinions regarding how the grant money should be spent.  You will hold an open board meeting to hear the opinions of all interested people from the community.  Then you will make your decision on how to spend the money.

### The Procedure

Follow these steps in your simulation:

1. The school board members open the meeting. They invite representatives from each of the three groups (teachers, parents, community leaders) to present their opinions on the proposals.

2. A representative from each group presents recommendations for how to reduce crime in schools.

3. The school board asks questions after each group's presentation. The board also invites questions from the audience.

4. The school board members vote to decide which proposals will be accepted and how much money will be spent for each one.

5. The school board reports its decision to everyone attending the meeting.

**"Attached to Crime" was first broadcast on *Morning Edition*, January 10, 1994. The reporter is Lynn Neary.**

# 5

# Their Old Lifestyle
# Is Worth Keeping

## ANTICIPATING THE ISSUE

### A. PREDICTING

Read the title and look at the photo. Discuss what you think the unit is about.

### B. THINKING AHEAD

In groups, discuss your answers to the following questions.

1. When immigrants move to a new country, what kind of life changes must they make? What parts of the new culture do they often adopt? What parts of their home culture do they often give up?

2. Describe the typical diet of people from your culture. How is it different from the typical American diet?

## II. ▷ VOCABULARY

Read the following sentences. The boldfaced words will help you understand the interview. Guess the meaning of these words from the context of the sentences. Then write a synonym or your own definition.

1. Many people are too busy to prepare dinner at home, so they end up *grabbing* something on their way home from work.

   _____

2. There's a *striking* similarity between Rachel and her mother. Their faces are almost identical!

   _____

3. Susan's daughter has a *unique* way of playing the piano. She sounds like no other musician we have heard.

   _____

4. Although it was difficult to stay on a diet, Sherry knew that her *reward* would soon be looking and feeling great!

   _____

5. Not everyone holds the *notion* that a low-fat diet is the best way to lose weight.

   _____

6. Gary had lost 25 pounds on his diet. *Ironically*, though, he gained it all back once he started eating three meals a day again.

   _____

7. In Japan and Korea, rice is a *staple*; it is served with almost every meal.

   _____

8. Yesterday's bread was *soaked* in eggs and milk, then fried in butter, to make a wonderful French toast breakfast!

   _____

9.  Ryan's mother never buys ***processed*** foods from the grocery store.  She always shops for healthy, organic foods in the health food shop.

_____

10. Jean's mother always served her children milk at dinner because she wanted them to get plenty of ***calcium***.

_____

11. Many people are getting the flu this winter, but I do not think it will become an ***epidemic***.

_____

12. ***Obesity*** has become a bigger problem in many countries around the world as people eat more junk food, exercise less, and prepare fewer meals at home.

_____

Match the words with their synonyms or definitions.

_____  1.  grab

_____  2.  striking

_____  3.  unique

_____  4.  reward

_____  5.  notion

_____  6.  ironically

_____  7.  staple

_____  8.  soak

_____  9.  processed

_____  10. calcium

_____  11. epidemic

_____  12. obesity

a.  a food that is needed and used all the time

b.  make something completely wet

c.  a mineral element that helps form teeth and bones

d.  prize; something given to someone for doing something good

e.  happening in a manner that is strange or unexpected

f.  state of being very overweight in an unhealthy way

g.  unusual or interesting enough to be noticed

h.  a large number of cases of a particular disease happening at the same time

i.  being the only one of its kind

j.  idea, belief, or opinion about something

k.  specially treated with substances to give food color or keep it fresh

l.  eat in a very short time

# III. LISTENING

## A. TASK LISTENING

Listen to the interview.  Find the answer to the following question.

How is the Mexican tortilla different from the American tortilla?

## B. LISTENING FOR MAIN IDEAS

Read the questions for each part.  Listen to the interview again.  It is divided into four parts.  You will hear a beep at the end of each part.  As you listen, circle the answer that expresses the main idea in that part.  Compare your answers with those of a partner.

**Part 1**    According to a study, what happens to people who migrate to the United States?

    a.  They eat better food.

    b.  They gain weight.

    c.  They have difficult experiences.

**Part 2**    What happens to people from India when they move to the United States?

    a.  They exercise the same amount and eat more.

    b.  They exercise less and eat more.

    c.  They exercise more and eat less.

**Part 3**    What do the data tell us about immigrants who come to the United States?

    a.  They arrive healthy.

    b.  They get help from the government.

    c.  They look more like Americans after several years.

> **Part 4**    Why is it hard to change immigrant families' eating habits?

   a.  They love eating "specialty foods."

   b.  They can only afford cheap snack foods.

   c.  They want to keep much of their old lifestyle.

## C.  LISTENING FOR DETAILS

Read the statements for Part 1.  Then listen to Part 1 again and decide whether the statements are true or false.  As you listen, write *T* or *F* next to each statement. Compare your answers with those of a partner.  If you disagree, listen again.

> **Part 1**

_____  1.  People who move to this country (the United States) exercise more.

_____  2.  A study was published in last week's *Journal of the American Medical Association.*

_____  3.  Dr. Mita Sanghavi Goel is an internist who works at a university.

_____  4.  She is studying migration to the United States.

_____  5.  Her parents grew up in India.

Repeat the same procedure for Parts 2–4.

> **Part 2**

_____  6.  Dr. Sanghavi Goel's parents were thin when they got married.

_____  7.  Her husband's parents were born in America.

_____  8.  Her parents drive and eat out more than they did in India.

_____  9.  There are big differences between her family's life in America and her family's life in India.

_____  10.  In India, her relatives cannot get as many fresh fruits and vegetables as in the United States.

_____  11.  In India, her relatives cook at home.

**Part 3**

_____ 12. Dr. Sanghavi Goel's experience is unique.

_____ 13. She and her colleagues analyzed data for 5,000 immigrants around the world.

_____ 14. They looked at health statistics from the government.

_____ 15. Immigrants look more like Americans after fifty years of living here.

_____ 16. A 5-foot 9-inch man is 11 pounds heavier than his recent immigrant counterpart.

_____ 17. After fifteen years of living in the United States, the average immigrant woman is nine pounds heavier than she was when she arrived.

**Part 4**

_____ 18. Marilyn Townsend directs a program to help immigrant families eat better.

_____ 19. Immigrants see these "specialty foods" as a reward.

_____ 20. Potato chips and snack foods are more expensive in the United States than in other countries.

_____ 21. Immigrants stop seeing them as luxury foods once they get here.

_____ 22. The corn tortilla is a staple in Mexico.

_____ 23. The corn tortilla is cooked in fat or oil.

_____ 24. In the United States, people are switching to corn tortillas.

_____ 25. The flour tortilla is very processed.

_____ 26. The epidemic of obesity in the United States cannot be controlled.

**LISTENING FOR INFERENCE**

Read the following questions.  Then listen to the excerpts from the interview.  Answer the questions.  Compare your answers with those of a partner.  Listen again if necessary.

### Excerpt 1

1. Why does she say, "and I hope I don't get myself into too much trouble with saying all this"?

   a.  She knows that she is not telling the truth about her family.

   b.  She thinks the interviewer will be unhappy with her answer.

   c.  She is afraid her family will be angry with her.

### Excerpt 2

2. What is the difference between the Mexican tortilla and the American tortilla?

   a.  The Mexican tortilla is healthier.

   b.  The American tortilla is healthier.

   c.  Both tortillas are equally healthy, but they are made with different ingredients.

## IV.  LOOKING AT LANGUAGE

### A.  USAGE:  Verbs of Perception

**Notice**

Listen to the excerpt from the interview.  Focus on the boldfaced words. What verb form do the verbs after *see* use?  What does this verb form mean?

I *see* my parents and my in-laws *driving* to the supermarket, often *eating* out, maybe *grabbing* an ice cream at night or *picking* up a candy bar at the checkout aisle or whatever it might be.

**Explanation**    The verb *see* is a verb of perception.  Verbs of perception are associated with the body's five senses: sight, hearing, taste, smell, and touch.  Here are some common verbs of perception:

| | | |
|---|---|---|
| feel | look at | see |
| hear | notice | smell |
| listen to | observe | watch |

The *-ing* form gives the idea that an activity is in progress, but not completed, when it is perceived.  The simple form gives the idea that the action was fully perceived from beginning to end.  Here is an example of the difference in meaning:

I see my parents driving to the supermarket.
(I see them at some point during their drive.)

I see my parents drive to the supermarket.
(I see them leave for the supermarket and arrive at the supermarket.  I watch the whole process of driving.)

## Exercise

Read the following sentences.  Write the *-ing* form or the simple form of the verbs in parentheses.  Remember that the *-ing* form gives the idea that an activity is in progress when it is perceived.

1.  If you observe people _____ (live) in the United States, you

    will notice that they often gain weight.

2.  When she looks at their wedding pictures, she sees her parents

    _____ (have) a good time and _____

    (look) healthy.

3.  Dr. Sanghavi Goel has observed immigrants _____ (change)

    their diet from the time of their arrival in the United States until now.

4.  If you went to India, you would see Dr. Sanghavi Goel's relatives

    _____ (shop) for fresh fruits and vegetables.

5.  When immigrants smell inexpensive "specialty foods"

    _____ (cook) in the streets, they want to eat them.

6.  If you are invited to an immigrant family's home in the United States, you may

    see them _____ (eat) a meal that is not as healthy as the

    traditional meals they ate in their home country.

7.  It is interesting to watch Mexicans _____ (make) a tortilla

    from start to finish: They grind the corn, soak it in lye liquid, and cook it without

    fat or oil.

8.  In the restaurant, the Mexican musicians came to our table.  I listened to them

    _____ (sing) a song from their home country.

## B.    PRONUNCIATION: Compound Nouns

**Notice**  Listen to the excerpts from the interview.  Focus on the underlined words.
Which of the two words is more stressed in each excerpt?  Why?

1.  It turns out many people who move to this country exercise less, eat more
    unhealthy food, and <u>gain weight</u>.

2.  Dr. Mita Sanghavi Goel is an internist at Northwestern University.  Her
    interests in looking at the link between migration to the U.S. and <u>weight
    gain</u> came from her own personal experience.

**Explanation**  In verb phrases, as in Excerpt 1, word stress varies.  Speakers may put the
stress on the verb or on the noun following it.  In Excerpt 1, the speaker
puts the stress on the verb *weight*.

A compound noun is a sequence of two or more words that together
function as a single noun.  As in Excerpt 2, the first word of a compound
noun is always stressed and is higher in pitch.  Note that some compound
nouns are spelled as one word, and all compound nouns are pronounced
like one word.

Sometimes the same combination of words can be either a compound noun or an adjective + noun sequence. The adjective can be a noun acting as an adjective, as in Excerpt 2. The difference in stress will alert a listener to the difference in meaning. For example, notice the stress change in the following two examples and how it affects meaning:

Have you ever seen a *blue*bird? (a particular bird species)

Have you ever seen a blue *bird*? (any bird that is blue in color)

In the compound noun, the stress falls on the first word. In the adjective + noun sequence, the stress falls on the second word.

## Exercise 1

Listen to the sentences. Focus on the stressed word. Circle *a* or *b* for the sentence you hear. Notice that the meaning changes with the stress change.

1. a. Bring in those hot *dogs*. (dogs that are hot)

   b. Bring in those *hot* dogs. (sausages served on a roll)

2. a. Can we find a quick short *stop*? (a stop to make while traveling)

   b. Can we find a quick *short*stop? (a baseball player)

3. a. Be careful not to burn yourself in that *hot* tub. (a large, heated tub that several people can sit in)

   b. Be careful not to burn yourself in that hot *tub*. (a regular bathtub that has hot water in it)

4. a. Joe's new green *house* gets very hot. (a house that is green)

   b. Joe's new *green*house gets very hot. (a glass house used for growing plants)

5. a. I need a better *sun*screen here. (cream you put on your skin to block the sun)

   b. I need a better sun *screen* here. (something that keeps the sun from shining into a particular space)

6. a. I don't like the taste of this *sour*dough. (dough that is made to taste sour)

   b. I don't like the taste of this sour *dough*. (dough that is no longer good and has a bad, sour taste)

7. a. Look straight at the *bulls*eye. (center of a target)

   b. Look straight at the bull's *eye*. (the eye of a bull)

8.  a. I haven't found the **green**belt yet.  (protected area of green land surrounding an urban area)

    b. I haven't found the green ***belt*** yet.  (green strip that is worn around the waist to keep pants on)

9.  a. He keeps his boat in the **New**port area.  (a town in the state of Rhode Island)

    b. He keeps his boat in the new ***port*** area.  (place where a new port has been built)

### Exercise 2

Work in pairs.  Take turns reading the sentences.  Focus on the stressed words.

## V.  FOLLOW-UP ACTIVITIES

### A.  DISCUSSION QUESTIONS

In groups, discuss your answers to the following questions.

1.  Which immigrants come to your country?  Do their eating patterns change when they move?  If so, how?

2.  How is the experience of immigrants to America different from the experience of their children who are born in America?  Do you think the eating habits are different between these two generations?  What about other cultural habits?

3.  Why is obesity becoming more of a problem in today's world?  What can be done about this problem?

## B.   VALUES CLARIFICATION:  School Lunches

### 1.   Take Notes to Prepare

By focusing on the lifestyle and diet changes of immigrants moving to the United States, you will be better able to complete the **values clarification** activity that follows.

Listen to the interview again.  Take notes on the lifestyle information.  Key phrases and some examples have been provided.

| Lifestyle outside the United States | Lifestyle in the United States |
|---|---|
| Appearance<br>• look fantastic<br>  in wedding pictures | Appearance |
| Habits | Habits<br>• exercise less |
| Available foods<br>• specialty foods are<br>  a reward | Available foods |

### 2.   Values Clarification

Work in groups.  One of the best ways to understand the typical diets of people in different countries is to look at the meals served to children in school.  Read the following descriptions of typical school lunches from different countries.  Then each person in the group ranks the lunches from 1 (most healthy) to 5 (least healthy).  Consider today's standards for healthy eating.  Share your rankings with your group.  Try to agree on one group ranking.  Then discuss which lunch you would enjoy eating most.  Are the healthiest meals the ones you most prefer?  Why or why not?

_____ **Japan**

A typical school lunch is a bowl of plain sticky rice, miso soup (often with tofu), assorted vegetables, some type of fish, a pickled salad or pickled seaweed, and a small bottle of milk. Sometimes there is a dessert: a cup of ice cream, gelatin, yogurt, or a piece of fruit.

_____ **United States**

Much of the food served in American schools is packaged. A typical lunch consists of a hamburger with french fries, shredded lettuce and pickles, chilled fruit, and cookies. Students are served milk.

_____ **Russia**

A typical meal has three courses and a fruit drink. Students start with an appetizer like borsht (a soup made out of beetroot, vegetables, and meat). This is followed by a main course of sausages or a cutlet (chopped meat mixed with egg and breadcrumbs, then fried) and mashed potatoes or boiled buckwheat. A dessert will often be biscuits or pancakes or syrki (chocolate covered cream cheese).

_____ **India**

Students are served hot meals. These are usually made with rice, lentils, dal (cooked cereal), a cooked vegetable curry, and yogurt or buttermilk. Students can also add a nonvegetarian side dish (typically chicken, mutton, or fish).

_____ **France**

A typical school lunch might be a grapefruit or a salad of raw vegetables (such as tomatoes, celery root, carrots), grilled chicken with green beans, a cheese course, and a dessert (usually a fruit). The meal is accompanied by water.

"Their Old Lifestyle Is Worth Keeping" was first broadcast on _Weekend All Things Considered_, December 15, 2004. The interviewer is Patricia Neighmond.

# 6

# The Bible Hospital

### A. PREDICTING

Read the title and look at the photo. Discuss what you think the unit is about.

### B. THINKING AHEAD

In groups, discuss your answers to the following questions.

1. Do you have anything that you would never throw away? Might someone else throw it away? Why do you keep it?

2. Do you have any special books? What books get used the most in your home?

3. Some families have businesses or work in certain professions and expect the younger generation to follow the same line of work. Is this true in your family? Why or why not? How will your work life be different from theirs?

## II.  VOCABULARY

Read the following sentences.  The boldfaced words will help you understand the
interview.  Guess the meaning of these words from the context of the sentences.
Then write a synonym or your own definition.

1.  When paintings are old and damaged, the museum carefully *restores* them.

   _____

2.  She is *rebinding* the dictionary because it was so old and used so often that it
    began to fall apart.

   _____

3.  The rug is very old and *worn*, so it needs to be repaired.

   _____

4.  Her favorite cookbook had been opened and closed so often that the *spine* was
    broken and pages were falling out.

   _____

5.  Many people will keep old photographs or objects for years just for *sentimental*
    reasons.

   _____

6.  To become members of the church, their children had to be *baptized*.

   _____

7.  At *confirmation*, her children officially promised their loyalty to the church.

   _____

8.  The coffee he spilled left *stains* on his white shirt.

   _____

9. Since his wife ***passed away*** two years ago, he has lived alone with his dog.

_____

10. With so much more free time in later life, many people take up new hobbies after they ***retire***.

_____

Match the words with their synonyms or definitions.

_____ 1. restore

_____ 2. rebind

_____ 3. worn

_____ 4. spine

_____ 5. sentimental

_____ 6. baptize

_____ 7. confirmation

_____ 8. stain

_____ 9. pass away

_____ 10. retire

a. a dirty spot that is hard to remove

b. repair something so that it is in its original condition

c. die

d. the part of a book that the pages are attached to

e. accept as a member of a Christian church after a religious ceremony in which the person is purified with water

f. showing emotions such as love and sadness too strongly

g. put papers together again and put into a cover

h. stop working, usually because of older age

i. being old and slightly damaged after being used a lot

j. a religious ceremony in which a person becomes a full member of a Christian church

# III.    LISTENING

## A.    TASK LISTENING

Listen to the interview.  Find the answer to the following question.

Which type of book, besides the Bible, is mentioned in this interview?

## B.  LISTENING FOR MAIN IDEAS

Read the questions for each part.  Listen to the interview again.  It is divided into four parts.  You will hear a beep at the end of each part.  As you listen, circle the answer that expresses the main idea in that part.  Compare your answers with those of a partner.

**Part 1**    What does Patrick Kirby do?

    a.  He works in a hospital.

    b.  He works in a book-repair shop.

    c.  He works in a library.

**Part 2**    How does Kirby restore a book?

    a.  He keeps all the book's leather.

    b.  He replaces all the book's leather.

    c.  He adds some new leather to the book.

**Part 3**    Why do people get their old books restored?

    a.  The old books have a special meaning.

    b.  The new books are more expensive.

    c.  The old books have stains.

**Part 4**    What is true about the Kirby family bookbinding business?

    a.  The business has always sewn books by hand.

    b.  Three generations have been involved in the business.

    c.  The family business may die.

## C. LISTENING FOR DETAILS

Read the statements for Part 1. Then listen to Part 1 again and decide whether the statements are true or false. As you listen, write *T* or *F* next to each statement. Compare your answers with those of a partner. If you disagree, listen again.

### Part 1

_____ 1. Patrick Kirby owns the Bible Hospital.

_____ 2. He does much of his work by hand.

_____ 3. He restores mostly private books.

_____ 4. Twenty percent of his work is rebinding bibles.

_____ 5. He restores about fifty large leather-bound bibles each year.

Repeat the same procedure for Parts 2–4.

### Part 2

_____ 6. Kirby will have to completely resew the book he is discussing.

_____ 7. The pages of the book are still together.

_____ 8. The spine of the book is split.

_____ 9. The old spine will be thrown away.

### Part 3

_____ 10. Hand bibles are expensive.

_____ 11. People often have dates written in their bibles.

_____ 12. The dates often reflect an important religious ceremony.

_____ 13. People get their cookbooks restored because old cookbooks were of better quality.

_____ 14. People want to preserve their checkmarks and tips in cookbooks.

> **Part 4**

     15. Kirby's father died in the 1960s.

     16. The Kirby family business has been going since 1935.

     17. Some of Kirby's equipment is as old as he is.

     18. Hand sewing a book would take about one hour.

     19. Hand-sewn jobs are better than machine-sewn jobs.

     20. Kirby may sell the business when he retires.

## D. LISTENING FOR INFERENCE

Read the following statements.  Then listen to the excerpt from the interview.  Decide whether you agree or disagree with the statements, based on the attitudes of the speakers.  Circle your answers.  Compare your answers with those of a partner. Listen again if necessary.

| | | |
|---|---|---|
| 1. Kirby admires his dad's work. | Agree | Disagree |
| 2. The interviewer thinks Kirby is old. | Agree | Disagree |
| 3. Kirby prefers doing things the old way. | Agree | Disagree |
| 4. Kirby is upset that his children are not interested in his business. | Agree | Disagree |

# IV. LOOKING AT LANGUAGE

## A. USAGE: Prefixes

> **Notice**

Listen to the excerpts from the interview.  Focus on the boldfaced words. What does the prefix *re-* mean?

1. He's a **restorer** of books, and he does much of the work by hand.

2. He **restores** books mostly for libraries, but about 20 percent of his work is **rebinding** private books, mainly bibles.

3. This one has to be **resewed***, completely **resewed.**

4. This piece of leather here will be lifted off the board here, pulled back about an inch or so, then we'll **reinsert** a new piece of leather in here.

**Explanation**

The prefix *re-* means "again." Prefixes are common in English. They can be added to adjectives, verbs, nouns, and roots to change their meaning. Notice how *re-* adds the meaning "again" to these words:

**re**do    **re**make    **re**establish    **re**unite

## Exercise 1

Complete the chart. Choose the correct definition of each prefix from the list below. Use the sample words to help you.

| reverse; undo | bad; wrong | put in, on | between |
| not | before | twice or two | stop; refuse |

| Prefix | Definitions | Sample words |
| --- | --- | --- |
| 1. **bi-** | twice or two | bicentennial; bilingual |
| | | |
| 2. **de-** | | defrost; depopulate |
| | | |
| 3. **dis-** | | disagree; disorder |
| | | |
| 4. **en- (em-)** | | enlist; empower |
| | | |

*can also be "resewn"

5. **in- (il-; im-; ir-)** _____    infinite; illiterate;
                                                 impossible; irregular

                                                 _____

6. **inter-**           _____      international; interracial

                                                 _____

7. **mis-**             _____      mistrust; misconduct

                                                 _____

8. **pre-**             _____      premature; prerecorded

                                                 _____

Work in pairs. Compare your answers with those of a partner. Then add new words
with the same prefix.

## Exercise 2

Read the following sentences. Choose the correct prefix for the given root word. Use
the information from the interview and the context of the sentence to help you.

1. Most of Kirby's customers _____ select the leather before
   rebinding a book.

   a. pre-        b. de-

2. The spine of a book that needs rebinding is usually _____
   connected from the rest of the book.

   a. inter-      b. dis-

3. Perhaps one of the reasons people go to the Bible Hospital is that their books are
   _____ replaceable.

   a. ir-         b. in-

4. According to the interviewer, cookbooks are _____
   dangered if people keep them in kitchens.

   a. en-         b. in-

5. People are rarely _____ satisfied with the work done at the Bible Hospital because Kirby puts so much care into repairing old books.

    a.  in-        b.  dis-

6. Many of the books that are brought in for binding are _____ colored.

    a.  dis-        b.  pre-

7. Children may _____ understand their parents' feelings about maintaining a family business.

    a.  mis-       b.  dis-

8. This old, torn journal was a _____ annual publication back in the 1950s.

    a.  pre-       b.  bi-

## B.  PRONUNCIATION: Prefixes and Suffixes

**Notice**  Listen to the excerpts from the interview. Focus on the boldfaced words. Is the primary stress on the prefix (*re-*) or the root word? Draw the stress marks.

1. He **restores** books mostly for libraries, but about 20 percent of his work is **rebinding** private books, mainly bibles.

2. This one has to be **resewed**, completely **resewed**.

3. This piece of leather here will be lifted off the board here, pulled back about an inch or so, then we'll **reinsert** a new piece of leather in here.

Listen to two more excerpts from the interview. Focus on the boldfaced words. Is the primary stress on the suffix (*-tion*) or the root word? Draw the stress marks.

4. That it was given to them when they were baptized or **confirmation** or something like that.

5. They just don't have **information** in the new ones like they do—like the old ones.

**Explanation** > In most words that add prefixes and suffixes, the stress does not change. The stress is on the base word. However, the stress changes to the syllable before the suffix with some suffixes: *-tion, -sion, -ic, -ical(ly), -ity, -ian, -ial, -graphy,* or *-logy.*

re ˋstore            restor ˋation
the ˋology           theo ˋlogical
senti ˋmental        sentimen ˋtality

## Exercise 1

Listen to the following sentences. Focus on the boldfaced words, which have a prefix or suffix. Put a stress mark on the syllable that receives primary stress in each word. Remember that some suffixes change the stress.

1. Kirby will repair a book when there is a ***separation*** of pages along its spine.

2. His shop ***remakes*** leather for the covers.

3. Kirby's shop has a lot of ***imitation*** leather.

4. Kirby knows that there is a ***psychological*** reason for preserving books.

5. Bibles are ***inexpensive***.

6. People take their books to the Bible Hospital because of ***sentimentality***.

7. People are ***unhappy*** when their cookbook starts to fall apart.

8. Kirby's children are ***uninterested*** in the business.

9. Kirby does not get a lot of ***publicity***, but his business has been in the family since 1939.

10. Kirby ***inherited*** his dad's business after his dad passed away.

11. He has not ***replaced*** his dad's old machinery.

12. People want to preserve the ***individuality*** of their marked-up books.

13. Kirby thinks that once he reaches ***retirement***, he will sell the business.

## Exercise 2

Work in pairs. Discuss the base word and whether or not the stress changes from the base word. Take turns reading the sentences. Focus on the stressed syllables.

## V. ▶ FOLLOW-UP ACTIVITIES

### A.  DISCUSSION QUESTIONS

In groups, discuss your answers to the following questions.

1.  What kinds of things do you save?  What kinds of things do you throw away?  Give examples.

2.  Some trades and professions are dying because children no longer continue their family's business.  Give examples from your country.

3.  What is the ideal relationship between people and their work?  Is it preferable to work in more anonymous or impersonal settings, such as in a large corporation?  Or is it preferable to work in more traditional or personal settings, such as in a family business?

### B.  CASE STUDY:  The Zimo Family

#### 1.  Take Notes to Prepare

By focusing on some of the issues presented in the interview, you will be better able to discuss the pros and cons of children continuing their family's business in the **case study** that follows.

Listen to the interview again.  Take notes on Patrick Kirby's bookbinding business. Key phrases and some examples have been provided.

What Kirby's business gives people

• sentimental value _____

_____

_____

The similarities between Kirby's business today and his father's business in 1939

• the stamper _____

_____

_____

The future of Kirby's business

• children aren't interested _____

_____

_____

✓ 2.  Case Study

You have listened to Patrick Kirby describe his bookbinding business.  His business will probably not continue because his children aren't interested in it.

Work in groups.  Read the case.  Discuss what decision Mike should make about his father's business.  Try to reach an agreement.  Take notes on your group's discussion.  You can use the chart on page 29 as a model for organizing your notes.  Then compare opinions with other groups.

The Zimo family has been in the hardware business for three generations.  In the 1940s Michael Zimo's father opened the first hardware store in a small town in New Jersey.  The store was very successful, and after his father passed away, Michael took over the business.

Michael has run the hardware store since 1962.  The business has been prosperous, and he is well respected in the community.  Two of his brothers have helped out with the business over the years.  As his children, Mike Jr. and Donna, grew up, they also helped out in the store.  Michael always thought that his son, Mike Jr., would eventually take over the family business.

After high school, Michael's children went away to college.  Mike Jr. went to Boston College and majored in music.  He dreamed of making it as a musician.  While at college, he played the guitar in a local band.  Unfortunately, he had trouble keeping up with his studies and had to drop out of college before completing his degree. When this happened, Mike's father persuaded him to come home and help out with the family business.

Mike decided to accept his father's offer, left Boston and his band, and went home to work with his father. The business was thriving, and he enjoyed the benefits of working with his family. He could take time off when he needed; he could work a fairly flexible schedule. Two years later, he got married and bought a house. His job enabled him to pay the mortgage on the house. Mike enjoyed working at the family hardware store, but somehow he felt unsettled: He had never fulfilled his dream of becoming a musician.

When Michael turned sixty-two, he was diagnosed with cancer. His doctors told him he probably had only months or less to live. Preparing for his death, he talked to his son about continuing the family business, but Mike's response wasn't totally positive. He felt conflicted. He wanted to support his father, but he couldn't imagine working at the hardware store all his life. He still wanted to pursue his music career. He also wanted to "make it on his own."

Mike's father couldn't believe that his son didn't care about the family business, the business he himself had dedicated his life to. He was hurt and disappointed that his son could abandon him. He was proud of what he had built and wanted his business to continue serving the community after he was gone. He also couldn't understand how his son could give up such a secure position. There was a lot of money to be made in this business. If Mike took the risk of pursuing a career in music, he might not succeed. And what's certain is that the family business would die.

Mike thought about his father's point of view; he didn't want to disappoint his father. But, at the same time, he wanted to pursue his own goals, to do something different. When he told his father that he felt frustrated that he had never really pursued his dream of becoming a musician, his father responded, "You gotta do what you gotta do."

"The Bible Hospital" was first broadcast on *All Things Considered*, April 27, 1994. The interviewer is Linda Wertheimer.

# The Baby Beeper

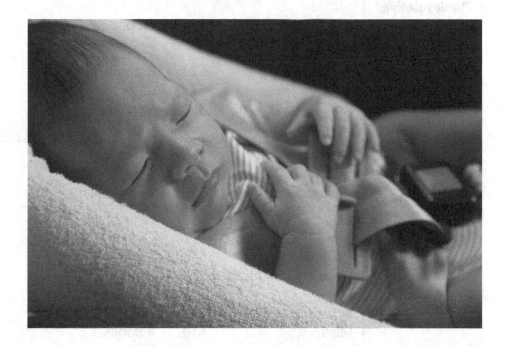

## A. PREDICTING

Read the title and look at the photo. Discuss what you think the unit is about.

## B. THINKING AHEAD

In groups, discuss your answers to the following questions.

1. Are students encouraged to enter science competitions in your country? If so, what kinds of programs exist? How do teachers get kids interested in science?

2. Look at the comparisons of international science scores on page 92. What do you notice? How do American students' science scores compare with those of students in other countries?

| INTERNATIONAL SCIENCE PERFORMANCE: Average science scores of 8th-grade students, by country: 2003 | | | | |
|---|---|---|---|---|
| **Rank relative to the United States** | **Country and score** | | | |
| Significantly higher | Singapore | 578 | Estonia | 552 |
| | Chinese Taipei | 571 | Japan | 552 |
| | Korea, Republic of | 558 | Hungary | 543 |
| | Hong Kong SAR | 556 | | |
| Not significantly different | Netherlands | 536 | Sweden | 524 |
| | United States | 527 | Slovenia | 520 |
| | Australia | 527 | New Zealand | 520 |
| Significantly lower | Lithuania | 519 | Macedonia | 449 |
| | Slovak Republic | 517 | Cyprus | 441 |
| | Belgium-Flemish | 516 | Bahrain | 438 |
| | Russian Federation | 514 | Palestinian National | |
| | Latvia | 512 | Authority | 435 |
| | Scotland | 512 | Egypt | 421 |
| | Malaysia | 510 | Indonesia | 420 |
| | Norway | 494 | Chile | 413 |
| | Italy | 491 | Tunisia | 404 |
| | Israel | 488 | Saudi Arabia | 398 |
| | Bulgaria | 479 | Morocco | 396 |
| | Jordan | 475 | Lebanon | 393 |
| | Moldova | 472 | Philippines | 377 |
| | Romania | 470 | Botswana | 365 |
| | Serbia | 468 | Ghana | 255 |
| | Armenia | 461 | South Africa | 244 |
| | Iran | 453 | | |

Source: National Center for Education Statistics, U.S. Department of Education.
(http://nces.ed.gov/programs/coe/2005/Section2/indicator12.asp)

## II. VOCABULARY

Read the following text. The boldfaced words will help you understand the interview. Guess the meaning of these words.

According to some studies, American students do not perform well in math and science in comparison to other students around the world. Studies have shown American students' performance in the middle grades to be especially weak.

In 1996, the Bayer Corporation, the National Science Foundation, and the Christopher Columbus Fellowship Foundation tried to find one solution to this problem. They created an *award* competition to make U.S. science education
1
more competitive at the middle school grades. The purpose of the competition is to *challenge* students to develop ideas to improve their communities.
2

The students can *dream up* any idea that involves science and technology.
3
The best way to *go about* this is to first identify an actual problem in their
4
community. The problem can be something that causes a disturbance to the community, such as car alarms. Or, it can be something even more serious, such as how to protect homes from earthquakes or hurricanes, which often lead to *fatal* results.
5

Once the students have selected a problem, they develop a solution using available technology. They might design a particular *device* to improve existing
6
products, such as wheelchairs, ladders, and toothbrushes. They might find better ways to *install* devices to improve product comfort or safety. For example,
7
students have found solutions to putting seats into cars that can be used by both tall and short people. Students have found a way to install seats into cars that are equally comfortable for short and tall drivers. They have also found ways to sound an alarm when the wrong combination is entered on a gun lock.

Each year, ten ***finalists*** are chosen from hundreds of entries.  Some of the
students are offered a chance to ***manufacture*** their inventions.  Some of the
inventions are even given ***patents*** by the U.S. government.  This protects their
ideas for future development.  For many students, the competition ***sets off*** a new
interest in science.  Many of the kids who participate in the competition go on to
study science in college.  They often say that it was the award competition that
started them in science careers.

Match the words in the text above with their definitions below.  Write the number of
each word next to its definition.

_____ test the skills or abilities of
someone or something

_____ people or teams who reach
the last part of a competition

_____ begin doing something

_____ special documents that say you
have the right to make or sell a
new invention or product and that
no one else is allowed to do so

_____ prize or money given to someone
for a special reason

_____ machine, tool, or other small
object that does a special job

_____ make goods in large numbers

_____ think of a plan or an idea,
especially something unusual

_____ resulting in someone's death

_____ makes something start happening

_____ put a piece of equipment
somewhere and connect it so
that it is ready to be used

## III.  LISTENING

### A.  TASK LISTENING

Listen to the interview.  Find the answer to the following question.

Who is interested in manufacturing the Baby Beeper?

### B.  LISTENING FOR MAIN IDEAS

Read the questions for each part.  Listen to the interview again.  It is divided into five parts.  You will hear a beep at the end of each part.  As you listen, circle the answer that expresses the main idea in that part.  Compare your answers with those of a partner.

**Part 1**    What did the seventh-graders do?

    a.  They created a competition.

    b.  They won first place in a competition.

    c.  They became finalists in a competition.

**Part 2**    Why did they invent the Baby Beeper?

    a.  Their parents asked them to do it.

    b.  They found out that many babies get left in cars.

    c.  The Las Vegas Fire Department needed it.

**Part 3**    How does the Baby Beeper work?

    a.  It makes a loud sound.

    b.  It rings a bell.

    c.  It moves your key chain.

**Part 4**    How did the girls come up with the idea?

    a.  They dreamed it up on their own.

    b.  They talked to engineers and parents.

    c.  They studied the way cars are built.

**Part 5**    Which has *not* been a result of their invention?

    a.  They manufactured their device.

    b.  They went to Disney World.

    c.  They went to the Kennedy Space Center.

## C.  LISTENING FOR DETAILS

Read the statements for Part 1.  Then listen to Part 1 again and decide whether the statements are true or false.  As you listen, write *T* or *F* next to each statement. Compare your answers with those of a partner.  If you disagree, listen again.

**Part 1**

_____  1.  The seventh-graders' idea has saved a lot of lives.

_____  2.  The Bayer/National Science Foundation Award competition is an annual event.

_____  3.  The competition challenges students to improve their homes with science and technology.

_____  4.  There are three members on the team.

_____  5.  The students go to middle school in Los Angeles.

Repeat the same procedure for Parts 2–5.

**Part 2**

_____  6.  The Baby Beeper is a device.

_____  7.  The girls think parents leave babies in cars accidentally.

_____ 8. If it is 90 degrees outside, the temperature can reach up to 120 degrees in a car in a half hour.

_____ 9. Leaving babies in cars can be fatal.

_____ 10. In 2000, the Las Vegas Fire Department rescued 519 babies from cars.

_____ 11. Five of those babies died.

## Part 3

_____ 12. The idea of the Baby Beeper is still only on paper.

_____ 13. When weight is on the pressure pad, it activates the transmitter.

_____ 14. The transmitter sends signals to a receiver.

_____ 15. The receiver is on the baby.

_____ 16. The baby's seat beeps when you walk away from your car.

## Part 4

_____ 17. The girls did not do a lot of research for their idea.

_____ 18. They surveyed parents for their ideas about the Baby Beeper.

_____ 19. The girls thought about having the device in the car or in the car seat.

_____ 20. The device would be movable.

## Part 5

_____ 21. Terry Ford works for TSI Alarm Companies.

_____ 22. The girls are trying to get a patent on their device.

_____ 23. There were 610 entries to the Bayer/National Science Foundation competition.

_____ 24. The girls could choose to go to one theme park in Disney World.

_____ 25. The girls catered a banquet in Orlando.

_____ 26. The girls went to the beach.

_____ 27. Their teacher and coach is Steve Loyd.

## D. LISTENING FOR INFERENCE

Read the following statements.  Then listen to the excerpts from the interview.  Circle *true* or *false* for each statement.  Compare your answers with those of a partner. Listen again if necessary.

**Excerpt 1**

1.  Most parents agreed on the price they          True    False
    would pay for the Baby Beeper.

**Excerpt 2**

2.  Most parents wanted a movable device          True    False
    rather than a device installed in the car.

**Excerpt 3**

3.  Going to the beach was more fun than          True    False
    going to the Kennedy Space Center.

# IV.  LOOKING AT LANGUAGE

## A.  USAGE: Real Conditionals

**Notice**    Listen to the excerpts from the interview.  Focus on the boldfaced verb forms.  What verb tense is used in each part of the sentence?  Can you explain why?

1.  There is a weight-sensitive pressure pad, which is wired to a transmitter, and ***when*** weight ***is*** on the pressure pad, it ***activates*** the transmitter, which sends signals to a receiver.

2.  And ***when*** you ***walk*** further away from your car, the receiver ***will begin*** to beep, alarming you that your baby's still in the car.

**Explanation**

Both excerpts are examples of conditional sentences. A conditional sentence usually consists of a conditional (*when/if*) clause and a result (main) clause. When a conditional clause talks about general truths, facts, or habits, both clauses are in the present tense. This is the case in Excerpt 1.

Note that the conditional clause often begins with *if* and sometimes with *whenever*. Excerpt 1 could also read:

> . . . and *if* weight *is* on the pressure pad, it *activates* the transmitter, which sends signals to a receiver.

> OR

> . . . and *whenever* weight *is* on the pressure pad, it *activates* the transmitter, which sends signals to a receiver.

Note also that the two clauses can be reversed without changing the meaning. Do not use a comma between the clauses when the result clause is first. The text above could read:

> It activates the transmitter whenever weight is on the pressure pad.

In Excerpt 2, the verb tenses in the two clauses are different. In this type of sentence, both the conditional clause and the result clause refer to something that can possibly happen in the future. The conditional clause is in the present tense and the result clause is in the future tense.

Note that the conditional clause often begins with *if* in these sentences. Excerpt 2 could also read:

> And *if* you *walk* further away from your car, the receiver *will begin* to beep, alarming you that your baby's still in the car.

Again, the two clauses can be reversed without changing the meaning.

**Exercise**

Read the following sentences. Decide whether the sentence is a statement about general truth, fact, or habit or a statement about future possibility. Write the correct tense of the verb in parentheses. Use the information in the interview to help you.

1. If middle-school-aged children _____ (present) their

   invention, the Bayer/National Science Foundation _____

   (enter) it into the annual competition.

2. Whenever the temperature _____ (reach) 90 degrees
   outside, it _____ (reach) 120 degrees in a car after a half
   hour.

3. According to the Las Vegas Fire Department, if they _____
   (rescue) hundreds of babies from cars, some of them _____
   (result) in death.

4. You _____ (send) a signal to a receiver when you
   _____ (activate) the Baby Beeper's transmitter.

5. If you _____ (research) the number of babies being left in
   cars, you _____ (find) that it is a very big problem.

6. Every year, there _____ (be) still only ten finalists, even
   when there _____ (be) hundreds of entries to the
   Bayer/National Science Foundation competition.

7. If you _____ (interview) parents about how much they
   would pay for the Baby Beeper, you _____ (get) a whole
   range of prices.

8. According to Kelsey and Rachelle, you _____ (visit) all of
   the theme parks when you _____ (win) a trip to Disney
   World.

## B.     PRONUNCIATION: -ed endings

**Notice** ▶   Listen to the excerpt from the interview. Focus on the pronunciation of the
            -ed endings in the boldfaced words. Do they sound similar or different? If
            they sound different, how are they different?

> We **researched**—we called the Las Vegas Fire Department and they
> told us that in the year 2000 they **rescued** 590 babies from cars, and
> five cases **resulted** in death. That was in Las Vegas alone.

**Explanation**     In English, the regular past tense *-ed* verb ending has three pronunciations: /t/, /d/, and /əd/ (or /ɪd/).  The pronunciation depends on the sound before the ending:

| VERB ENDINGS | PAST TENSE PRONUNCIATION | EXAMPLES |
|---|---|---|
| verbs ending in a voiceless consonant sound (but not /t/) | past tense ending pronounced as /t/ | research → researched<br>like → liked<br>beep → beeped<br>finish → finished |
| verbs ending in a vowel or a voiced consonant sound (but not /d/) | past tense ending pronounced as /d/ | rescue → rescued<br>challenge → challenged<br>improve → improved<br>enter → entered |
| verbs ending in /t/ or /d/, the past tense ending is pronounced as /əd/ or /ɪd/. | extra syllable is added to the verb | result → resulted<br>compete → competed<br>transmit → transmitted<br>remind → reminded |

## Exercise 1

Listen to the excerpts from the interview.  Focus on the pronunciation of the *-ed* ending of each underlined word.  Write the words in the correct category in the chart below.  Compare answers with a partner.  Listen again if necessary.

1.  Their idea and the invention that <u>followed</u> have <u>earned</u> them a place as finalists in the Bayer/National Science Foundation Award competition.

2.  Rachelle, what is it that you've <u>invented</u> and why?

3.  Well, this contest that you're entering, it <u>required</u> you not just to dream up this idea, but you had to do a lot of research about how babies' lives could be <u>saved</u> and if people would really buy this invention.

4.  And we <u>talked</u> to a lot of people, like different engineers and different parents to see what their ideas were.

5.  Like, we <u>called</u> parents and we <u>tried</u> to see what they think would be useful for a parent to use in, like, the way should we have it in the car, or should we have it in its own car seat, and stuff like that, so.

6. So the device would be movable, and it wouldn't have to be <u>installed</u> in the car seat.

7. Go to all the theme parks. There's banquets that we go to the whole time we're there, and it's really nice—<u>catered</u> and all this stuff.

8. They <u>joined</u> us from member station KNPR in Las Vegas.

| /t/ | /d/ | /əd/ or /ɪd/ |
|-----|-----|-----|
|  |  |  |
|  |  |  |
|  |  |  |

### Exercise 2

Work in pairs. Take turns reading the sentences above. Focus on the -ed endings.

## V. FOLLOW-UP ACTIVITIES

### A. DISCUSSION QUESTIONS

In groups, discuss your answers to the following questions.

1. The girls found out that in one year, 590 babies had to be rescued from cars in Las Vegas alone. Why do you think people leave babies in cars? Why might people need to be reminded that a baby is still in the car? What does this say about modern life?

2. The purpose of the Bayer/National Science Foundation Award is to help get kids interested in science. Do young students in your home country need to be encouraged to study science? Why or why not?

3. Pretend that you are in a science competition similar to the one in this interview. What would you invent? Remember: It can be something simple that helps with an everyday problem.

## B.   Values Clarification: Scientific Inventions

### 1.   Take Notes to Prepare

By focusing on the problems and solutions that led to the invention of the Baby Beeper, you will be better able to rank it among the other competition finalists in the **values clarification** activity that follows.

Listen to the interview again. Take notes on the problem, solution, and award for the Baby Beeper. Key phrases and some examples have been provided.

#### Problem

• Parents accidentally leave children in cars .

_____

_____

_____

#### Solution

• Loud beep warns you—baby is in car.

_____

_____

_____

#### Award

• Trip to Disney World

_____

_____

_____

### 2.   Values Clarification

Work in groups. Read the descriptions of inventions from other middle school finalists who competed for the Bayer/National Science Foundation Award that year.

Pretend that you are the judges. Which proposals help make a community a better place to live? How would you award these proposals? Rank the proposals from 1 (most important) to 5 (least important). Try to agree on one group ranking.

### _____ The Wheelchair Braking System

_Problem:_ Wheelchairs are difficult to control when they go down ramps. People can get hurt.

_Solution:_ The students used trigonometry to determine the amount of force needed for the brake to slow down the wheelchair on standard ramps. These ramps slope at a grade of 12 feet for every 1 foot of height. Their solution was the Pendulum Braking System.

### _____ The Stopping Cart

_Problem:_ Runaway shopping carts (carts that roll away by themselves) are a common problem in the parking lots of many grocery stores and large chain stores. These runaway carts damage customers' cars. One store manager reports that his chain paid an average of $5,000 per store in their 1,600 stores across the country for runaway carts.

_Solution:_ The students interviewed scientists, engineers, chain-store managers and customers to find a solution. They developed a set of brakes for the carts. The brakes disengage easily when the staff collects them in parking lots to return them to the store.

### _____ The Ladder Stabilizer

_Problem:_ Each year more than 90,000 people are taken to hospitals because of ladder accidents. These accidents are often caused by a person's shift in the center of gravity when using a ladder. For example, if someone is painting or doing repairs, he or she may reach out and away from the ladder, lose his or her balance, and fall.

_Solution:_ The students developed L-shaped, adjustable stabilizers for ladders. The stabilizers can stop ladders from tipping. This reduces accidents.

### _____ The Baby Beeper

_Problem:_ Every year more and more babies are being left in cars. In one year alone, the Las Vegas Fire Department responded to calls for almost 600 babies being left in cars. Five of these cases resulted in death.

*Solution:* The students surveyed community members to see whether they would use a car seat alarm. They received a positive response. The students then created a system by which a pad beneath the baby seat activates a transmitter. This transmitter keeps in contact with a receiver on the parent's or caregiver's key chain. If that person goes more than 20 feet from the car, it beeps to alert him or her that the child has been left in the car.

_____    **The Quiet Car Alarm**

*Problem:* People are tired of hearing car alarms going off in their neighborhoods. They often cannot sleep or concentrate on what they are doing when they hear these alarms.

*Solution:* The students looked for a way to let car owners know that their car alarms had been activated—but without the loud noise. They studied pagers and car alarm systems. They discovered that by placing a transmitter in the car, they could send a page to the car owner when the car alarm went off. This silent communication would alert the owner to the emergency without disturbing the neighborhood.

**"The Baby Beeper"** was first broadcast on *All Things Considered,* June 9, 2002. The interviewer is Korva Coleman.

# 8

# If It Smells Like Fish, Forget It

## 1. ANTICIPATING THE ISSUE

### A. PREDICTING

Read the title and look at the photo. Discuss what you think the unit is about.

### B. THINKING AHEAD

In groups, discuss your answers to the following questions.

1. Do you eat fish? Do you ever buy or cook fresh fish? If so, describe what you do.

2. Do you usually shop for fresh food? How do you decide whether certain foods are fresh? Give some examples.

3. What advertising techniques do supermarkets use to encourage you to buy food? How do they make food look fresher than it really is? Give some examples.

## II. ▷ VOCABULARY

### Exercise 1

Look at the drawing of a fish.  Read the vocabulary and definitions below.  Then label each part of the fish.

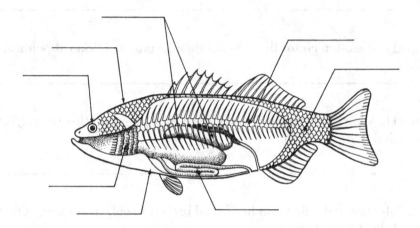

**backbone:** spine; line of bones down the middle of the back

**belly:** stomach; bulging part of the body

**eye:** organ of sight

**scales:** small, flat pieces of hard skin that cover the bodies of fish

**viscera:** internal organs of the body

**slime:** sticky substance on the surface of fish

**gill:** organ through which fish breathe

**guts:** intestines; bowels

**Exercise 2**

Read the following sentences. The boldfaced words will help you understand the interview. Guess the meaning of these words from the context of the sentences. Then write a synonym or your own definition.

1. Near the harbor, you can hear the *fishmongers* calling out the names of the fish they're trying to sell.

   _____

2. People often *chant* the name of their favorite politician at political rallies.

   _____

3. He knows Italy very well, so he gave me some good *tips* on which towns to visit during my vacation.

   _____

4. She tasted the first dish her friend had ever cooked and said, "Oh, this is *yucky*. I don't think I can eat it!"

   _____

5. A fish must be *slitted* and cleaned out before you can cook it.

   _____

6. Sometimes when paper gets old, the ends *curl* up.

   _____

7. The grass looks *patchy*; some parts are so green, and some parts are old and dry.

   _____

8. That food is *spoiled*. It's been in the refrigerator too long. Now we won't be able to eat it.

   _____

9. When the archaeologists discovered the dinosaur bones, they were surprised that the whole skeleton had remained *intact*.

_____

10. He hadn't been in the sun all summer, so his skin was *pale*, unlike the other tanned tourists.

_____

Match the words with their synonyms or definitions.

_____ 1. fishmonger          a. make a straight, narrow cut in something

_____ 2. chant               b. repeat a word or phrase many times

_____ 3. tips                c. become bad; decay

_____ 4. yucky               d. not broken, damaged, or spoiled; complete

_____ 5. slit                e. unpleasant or disgusting

_____ 6. curl                f. irregular; different from the surrounding parts; spotty

_____ 7. patchy

_____ 8. spoil               g. having light color; not bright

_____ 9. intact              h. twist; form a curved shape

_____ 10. pale               i. helpful advice; suggestions

                             j. person who sells fish

# III. LISTENING

## A. TASK LISTENING

Listen to the interview. Find the answer to the following question.

Which part of the fish is, surprisingly, *not* a great indicator of how fresh a fish is? See the fish vocabulary on page 107 if you need help.

## B.   LISTENING FOR MAIN IDEAS

Read the questions for each part.  Listen to the interview again.  It is divided into five parts.  You will hear a beep at the end of each part.  As you listen, circle the answer that expresses the main idea in that part.  Compare your answers with those of a partner.

**Part 1**     What will we learn from this interview?

a. how to shop for fish

b. how to distinguish different types of fish

c. how to choose a fish man (supplier)

**Part 2**     How should a fish look when you buy it?

a. bloody

b. not fat

c. flat

**Part 3**     How should a fish feel when you buy it?

a. slimy

b. icy

c. patchy

**Part 4**     Which part of the fish is a good indicator of freshness?

a. the eyes, when the fish has been on ice

b. the gills, when the fish is intact

c. the guts, when the fish has been slitted

**Part 5**    What should a quality fish operation smell like?

    a.  a good fish environment

    b.  a fishy environment

    c.  nothing

## C.  LISTENING FOR DETAILS

Read the statements for Part 1.  Then listen to Part 1 again and decide whether the statements are true or false.  As you listen, write *T* or *F* next to each statement. Compare your answers with those of a partner.  If you disagree, listen again.

**Part 1**

\_\_\_\_\_   1.  Every red-blooded American knows how to buy fresh fish.

\_\_\_\_\_   2.  Even vegetarians should listen to this interview.

\_\_\_\_\_   3.  The interview takes place in Seattle.

\_\_\_\_\_   4.  Some customers come for the show more than the fish.

\_\_\_\_\_   5.  The fishmongers play football while they sell fish.

\_\_\_\_\_   6.  Brian Poor, a local chef, asks the fishmongers to inspect the fish for him.

Repeat the same procedure for Parts 2–5.

**Part 2**

\_\_\_\_\_   7.  Brian Poor says the backbone area is the first place to look to see if a fish is fresh.

\_\_\_\_\_   8.  He does not want blood on the backbone.

\_\_\_\_\_   9.  Brown blood is a sign of an old fish.

\_\_\_\_\_  10.  A fish with no blood may have been washed.

\_\_\_\_\_  11.  A just-slitted and cleaned fish has a flat belly.

\_\_\_\_\_  12.  An older fish's belly curls in on itself.

\_\_\_\_\_  13.  A fresh fish looks like it still has the viscera in it.

## Part 3

____ 14. The interviewer does not like slimy fish.

____ 15. Melting ice will keep the slime on a fish.

____ 16. Slime is necessary for a fish's life.

____ 17. The slimier the fish, the better.

____ 18. The more scales there are on the fish, the less the fish has been handled.

## Part 4

____ 19. If a fish has been iced up, the eyes can be a good indicator of freshness.

____ 20. Never buy a cloudy-eyed fish.

____ 21. A spoiled fish sometimes has glassy eyes.

____ 22. The gills on a fish should be bloody.

____ 23. Most gutted fish do not have gills intact.

____ 24. The gills on a fish should be pale.

## Part 5

____ 25. Brian Poor sniffs a fish to judge its freshness.

____ 26. If a fish market smells like fish, you should tell the people working there.

____ 27. Fresh fish do not smell.

## D. LISTENING FOR INFERENCE

This interview gives tips for buying fish.  Read the statements summarizing each tip.
Then listen to the excerpts from the interview.  How important is the tip, according to
the speakers?  Circle a number from 1 (not important) to 5 (extremely important).
Compare your answers with those of a partner.  Listen again if necessary.

**Excerpt 1**

1.  The fish should have blood on the backbone.

| Not necessarily important | Important | Extremely important |
|---|---|---|
| 1          2          3          4          5 | | |

**Excerpt 2**

2.  The fish's belly shape should not be flat.

| Not necessarily important | Important | Extremely important |
|---|---|---|
| 1          2          3          4          5 | | |

**Excerpt 3**

3.  The fish should be slimy.

| Not necessarily important | Important | Extremely important |
|---|---|---|
| 1          2          3          4          5 | | |

**Excerpt 4**

4.   The fish should have scales intact.

| Not necessarily important | Important | Extremely important |
|---|---|---|
| 1          2          3          4          5 | | |

**Excerpt 5**

5.   The fish should have clear eyes.

| Not necessarily important | Important | Extremely important |
|---|---|---|
| 1          2          3          4          5 | | |

# IV. LOOKING AT LANGUAGE

## A. USAGE: Double Comparatives

**Notice**  Listen to the excerpt from the interview. Focus on the underlined words. Can you explain what the speaker means?

ZWERDLING: So, Brian Poor, the more slime the better.

POOR: <u>The more slime, the better.</u>

ZWERDLING: OK. What about scales? Sometimes people say— Any clue?

POOR: <u>The more they are handled, the more scales they lose.</u>

**Explanation**  Brian Poor is using a double comparative to show a cause-and-effect relationship. He is saying that:

1. If a fish has slime, it is a fresher (better) fish. (So we want to shop for slimy fish.)

2. If people handle fish, the fish lose their scales. (So we want to shop for fish that still have their scales.)

Here is the structure for a double comparative:

| *the* | COMPARATIVE FORM (CAUSE) | *the* | COMPARATIVE FORM (EFFECT) |
|---|---|---|---|
| The | more slime (there is), | the | better (it is). |
| The | more they are handled, | the | more scales they lose. |
| The | more a fish smells, | the | less fresh it is. |

## Exercise 1

Read the following sentences.  Write the correct double comparative forms of the adjectives in parentheses.  Use the chart on page 114 to help you.

1.  It's not easy to shop for melons, but most people think that

    _____ the smell, _____ the melon.
    (sweet)                        (delicious)

2.  More and more people are concerned about the fat content in hamburger meat

    these days.  Usually, _____ the color,
    (red)

    _____ the meat.
    (lean)

3.  I only buy peaches in the summer.  And _____ the peach,
    (ripe)

    _____ it tastes.
    (good)

4.  Not everyone agrees, but the French generally think that for cheese,

    _____ the smell, _____ its taste.
    (strong)                        (delicious)

5.  Red wine gets better over time.  _____ you store it,
    (long)

    _____ it tastes when you drink it.
    (smooth)

6.  Good bread should be eaten the day it's bought.  _____ you
    (long)

    keep it, _____ it will taste.
    (fresh)

## Exercise 2

Rewrite the following sentences.  Use cause-and-effect comparative sentences.

1.  When a banana peel is green, the banana is not yet ripe.

    *The greener the peel, the less ripe the banana.*

2.  When vegetables are grown to be very large, they don't have much taste.

    _____

3. When fruit is of good quality, the cost is usually high.

_____

4. When fruit juice is natural, the taste is not so sweet.

_____

5. When raspberries look beautiful, they taste delicious.

_____

6. When food has additives, it lasts longer.

_____

7. When its interior is soft, an avocado is ripe.

_____

## B. PRONUNCIATION: /s/ versus /ʃ/

**Notice** ▷ Listen to the excerpts from the interview. Focus on the two sounds of the boldfaced letters. How are the sounds similar? How are they different?

1. ZWERDLING: Now **s**ometimes I go into a fi**sh s**tore or a fi**sh** counter at the **s**upermarket, and I pick up the fi**sh**, and it'**s s**limy, and I think, ugh.

   POOR: You **sh**ould go, "Hooray."

   PETERSON: The melting i**ce** alone, will remove the **s**lime from the fi**sh**. The **s**lime is their clothing. It in**s**ulate**s** them when they're in the water, **s**o they don't die of exposure. They have to have it.

2. ZWERDLING: Ohhh. . . . But **s**till, it's a real ni**ce** fre**sh** fi**sh**.

   PETERSON: Yeah.

   POOR: It'**s** a good one. It can be a good one. You can—I have **s**een fi**sh** that were completely **s**poiled with gla**ss**y clear eyes because they had never **s**een i**ce**; they were in the trunk of a fi**sh**erman's car.

**Explanation**    In the excerpts, the sounds /s/ and /ʃ/ are both voiceless. If we touch our throat when we pronounce these sounds, there is no vibration. This is how the sounds are similar.

The articulation of the two sounds, however, is different. For the /s/ sound, the tip of our tongue is raised, pointing near, but not touching, the gum ridge behind our upper front teeth.

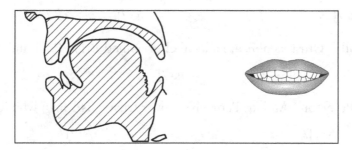

For the /ʃ/ sound, the tip of our tongue is pulled back more than it is in the /s/ position. We round our lips slightly.

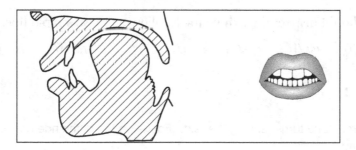

### Exercise 1

Listen to the introduction of the interview. Focus on the pronunciation of the boldfaced letters. Circle the correct symbol.

Now we're going to learn **s**omething that every red-blooded American

/s/ /ʃ/

**sh**ould know—how to **sh**op for fre**sh** fi**sh**. If you're a **s**trict vegetarian, li**s**ten

/s/ /ʃ/              /s/ /ʃ/    /s/ /ʃ/  /s/ /ʃ/      /s/ /ʃ/            /s/ /ʃ/

anyway, and you can pa**ss** the information on to your friends. Our cla**ss**room is

/s/ /ʃ/

a seafood stall called Pike Pla**ce** Fi**sh** at the Pike Pla**ce** Market near **S**eattle's

/s/ /ʃ/ /s/ /ʃ/ /s/ /ʃ/ /s/ /ʃ/ /s/ /ʃ/ /s/ /ʃ/

harbor. A lot of customers come here not **s**o much for the food, but for the **sh**ow.

/s/ /ʃ/ /s/ /ʃ/ /s/ /ʃ/

The fi**sh**mongers chant every order and to**ss** trout and **s**almon to each other like

/s/ /ʃ/ /s/ /ʃ/ /s/ /ʃ/

footballs. Our teachers are a local **ch**ef named Brian Poor and the **s**tall's manager,

/s/ /ʃ/ /s/ /ʃ/

John Peterson. And, as Poor **s**ays, never tru**s**t a fi**sh** man who look**s** you deep in

/s/ /ʃ/ /s/ /ʃ/ /s/ /ʃ/ /s/ /ʃ/ /s/ /ʃ/

the eyes and **s**ays, "Of course, all these fi**sh** came in just thi**s** morning." He **s**ays

/s/ /ʃ/ /s/ /ʃ/ /s/ /ʃ/ /s/ /ʃ/ /s/ /ʃ/ /s/ /ʃ/

you **sh**ould inspect the fi**sh** yourself following these **s**imple tip**s**.

/s/ /ʃ/ /s/ /ʃ/ /s/ /ʃ/ /s/ /ʃ/ /s/ /ʃ/ /s/ /ʃ/

## Exercise 2

Work in pairs. Take turns reading the text. Focus on the difference between the /s/ and /ʃ/ sound.

## Just for Fun

Work in pairs. Take turns reading the tongue twisters. Focus on the difference between the /s/ and /ʃ/ sound.

She sells seashells by the seashore.
The seashells that she sells are seashells I'm sure.

I saw Susie sitting in a shoe shine shop.
Where she sits she shines, and where she shines she sits.

# V.  FOLLOW-UP ACTIVITIES

## A.  DISCUSSION QUESTIONS

In groups, discuss your answers to the following questions.

1. Is the freshness of food important to you?  Will the information from this interview change the way you shop for fish or for any fresh food?  If so, how?

2. What tips would you give for buying fresh foods in your country?

3. Describe a product that you purchased and that you now regret purchasing. What do you know now that you should have known when you bought it?  What advice would you give someone buying a similar product?

## B.  ADVICE: Shopping Tips

### 1.  Take Notes to Prepare

By focusing on how to buy fresh fish, you will be better able to offer **advice** in the activity that follows.

Listen to the interview again.  Take notes on the important considerations in choosing fresh fish.  Key phrases and some examples have been provided.

Who should inspect the fish

• the customer _____

_____

_____

_____

_____

Blood

• blood should be on the backbone _____

_____

_____

_____

_____

Belly shape

• nice belly shape _____

_____

_____

_____

_____

Outside of a fish

• the more slime, the better _____

_____

_____

_____

Eyes

• cloudy eyes not an indication of freshness _____

_____

_____

_____

_____

Gills

• _farm-raised fish come intact_ _____

_____

_____

_____

_____

Requirements of a quality fish supplier

• _no smell when you sniff_ _____

_____

_____

_____

_____

 2.  Advice

In the interview, you heard about how to buy fresh fish.  It is not always easy to
know what to look for when buying a product you do not know well.

**The Product**

Work in groups.  Choose a product that you are familiar with.  You can choose
one of the products below, or you may choose one of your own.

**Food**

- chicken
- melons
- tomatoes
- grapefruits

**Home Appliances**

- coffeemakers
- toasters
- washers/dryers

### Electronics

- computers
- DVD players
- stereos
- cell phones
- mp3 players

### Vehicles

- used cars
- new cars
- motorcycles

### Sports Equipment

- sneakers
- skis
- tennis rackets
- exercise machines

### Clothing

- designer versus imitation

### The Procedure

Create a list of tips for buying the product. Consider the following points:

- What should it look like on the outside?

- What should it be made of on the inside?

- Which parts are most important?

- Which dealers/suppliers are the best?

- Who should give you advice on buying the product?

Present your tips to the class.

**"If It Smells Like Fish, Forget It"** was first broadcast on *All Things Considered*, November 19, 1994. The interviewer is Daniel Zwerdling.

# 9

# Home Instead

## I. ANTICIPATING THE ISSUE

### A. PREDICTING

Read the title and look at the photo. Discuss what you think the unit is about.

### B. THINKING AHEAD

In groups, discuss your answers to the following questions.

1. A nursing home is a place where people who are too old or sick to take care of themselves can live. Are nursing homes popular in your country? Do families ever put their parents in nursing homes if they cannot take care of them themselves?

2. What are the advantages and disadvantages to having older or sick people living at home?

## II. ▶ VOCABULARY

Read the following sentences. The boldfaced words will help you understand the report. Guess the meaning of these words from the context of the sentences. Then write a synonym or your own definition.

1. Busy parents are finding it more and more difficult to **manage** family and work life.

   _____

2. It is important for older people to have **companionship** so they do not get lonely.

   _____

3. McDonald's is the largest fast-food **franchise** business in the world.

   _____

4. Today more and more **seniors** are living well into their nineties.

   _____

5. The business was so **profitable** that it doubled its earnings in less than one year.

   _____

6. The pizza delivery man had to be **buzzed into** the apartment building before he took the elevator to the eighteenth floor.

   _____

7. Unable to walk because of her **MS**, Marie had to use a wheelchair.

   _____

8. Everyone said Mark's mother was a **gem** because she had raised many children, cooked wonderful meals for her family, and still volunteered at the local hospital.

   _____

9. Joanne has been a teacher for over forty years because she finds her work with children to be so ***rewarding***.

_____

10. Working in that restaurant is a great part-time job if you want to earn a few extra ***bucks***.

_____

**Match the words with their synonyms or definitions.**

_____  1.  manage

_____  2.  companionship

_____  3.  franchise

_____  4.  senior

_____  5.  profitable

_____  6.  buzz in

_____  7.  MS

_____  8.  gem

_____  9.  rewarding

_____  10.  buck

a.  being with someone so that you have someone to talk to and do not feel lonely

b.  making money by selling things or doing business

c.  multiple sclerosis; a serious disease that gradually destroys your nerves, making you weak and unable to walk

d.  dollar

e.  someone or something that is very special

f.  permission that a company gives to a person or group to sell the company's products or services

g.  succeed in doing something difficult, such as dealing with a problem, or living in a difficult situation

h.  making you feel happy and satisfied

i.  allow to enter through a locked door because someone inside presses a button

j.  older person, especially someone over the age of sixty-five

# III. ▷ LISTENING

## A. TASK LISTENING

Listen to the report.  Find the answer to the following question.

How many elderly or disabled people does Home Instead serve?

## B. LISTENING FOR MAIN IDEAS

Read the questions for each part.  Listen to the report again.  It is divided into five parts. You will hear a beep at the end of each part.  As you listen, circle the answer that expresses the main idea in that part.  Compare your answers with those of a partner.

**Part 1**    What have more elderly people been doing over the past decade?

    a.  going into nursing homes

    b.  moving in with their families

    c.  getting help to manage at home

**Part 2**    How did Paul Hogan get his idea for his own franchise?

    a.  His parents gave him the idea.

    b.  He learned about it at the University of Nebraska.

    c.  He realized what his family was doing for his grandmother.

**Part 3**    Why did Hogan realize his business would be successful?

    a.  It took his whole family to keep his grandmother in the home environment.

    b.  Most home-care services were profitable.

    c.  Franchises were becoming popular abroad.

**Part 4**    What role does Roberta Ryan play in Betty Ranigan's life?

    a.  She gave her surgery in October.

    b.  She shops and cleans for her.

    c.  She takes her on trips to Canada.

**Part 5**    How does Home Instead get good workers?

    a.  It pays them a high salary.

    b.  It offers rewarding work.

    c.  It hires them from home-care providers.

## C.  LISTENING FOR DETAILS

Read the questions for Part 1.  Then listen to Part 1 again.  As you listen, circle the best answers.  Compare your answers with those of a partner.  If you disagree, listen again.

**Part 1**

1. When do many elderly people *not* want to go to nursing homes?
   a.  when they are sick
   b.  when they have trouble doing everyday tasks
   c.  when their families move away

2. Home medical care is _____.
   a.  cheap
   b   affordable
   c.  expensive

3. What does the new home-care industry do?
   a.  It helps people move out of their home.
   b.  It takes control of the home.
   c.  It provides companionship in the home.

Repeat the same procedure for Parts 2–5.

### Part 2

4. Paul Hogan's parents _____.

   a. have always lived with his grandmother

   b. lived in Omaha, Nebraska

   c. could not care for his grandmother

5. What did the family do for the grandmother?

   a. cooked her meals

   b. bought her medications

   c. kept her connected to her community

6. When did she have her hair appointment?

   a. Friday at one o'clock

   b. Tuesday at noon

   c. every Sunday

7. When Hogan was in his late twenties, he did *not* have _____.

   a. a degree in finance

   b. a job at a large housecleaning company

   c. his own franchise chain

### Part 3

8. How many grandchildren did Hogan's grandmother have?

   a. 12

   b. 50

   c. 51

9. What did Hogan do in 1994?

   a. He quit his job.

   b. He married his wife.

   c. He went to work at Home Instead.

10. Which service does Home Instead offer?

   a. cleaning

   b. church service

   c. hairdressing

11. How many franchises does Home Instead have in the United States?

   a. 425

   b. dozens

   c. 25,000

**Part 4**

12. How old is Betty?

   a. 40

   b. 50

   c. 60

13. What does Roberta do for Betty every week?

   a. She comes to make her coffee.

   b. She brings her son for a visit.

   c. She runs errands for her.

14. When did they go to New Hampshire?

   a. last Sunday

   b. almost three weeks ago

   c. three weeks ago

15. Whose play did she see?

    a. her cousin's

    b. her husband's

    c. her granddaughter's

**Part 5**

16. How much does Roberta make in her job?

    a. twenty-two dollars an hour

    b. twenty dollars an hour

    c. ten dollars an hour

17. Which does *not* describe the people who work for Jack Cross, a local franchise owner?

    a. funny

    b. reliable

    c. friendly

18. What kind of experience do the workers have for this job?

    a. They have been trained by Home Instead.

    b. They have taken care of a relative.

    c. They have worked with great people.

19. Home-care providers are now licensed _____.

    a. in most states

    b. in more than a dozen states

    c. across the industry

## D.  LISTENING FOR INFERENCE

Read the questions.  Then listen to the excerpts from the report.  Circle the words that best express the speaker's feelings.  Compare your answers with those of a partner. Listen again if necessary.

**Excerpt 1**

1.  How does Paul Hogan feel?

| | | | | |
|---|---|---|---|---|
| happy | frustrated | committed | sad | proud |
| responsible | angry | serious | confused | excited |

**Excerpt 2**

2.  How does Betty Ranigan (the person being cared for) feel?

| | | | | |
|---|---|---|---|---|
| happy | frustrated | committed | sad | friendly |
| content | angry | serious | confused | secure |

# IV.  LOOKING AT LANGUAGE

## A.  USAGE: Idioms

**Notice** ▷   Listen to the excerpts from the report.  Focus on the boldfaced words. Guess their meaning from the context of the excerpts.  Discuss your ideas with a partner.

1.  When Paul Hogan's grandmother got too old to live at home by herself, his parents decided to take her in.  After all, they lived just ***up the*** same ***road*** in Omaha, Nebraska.

2.  And it gradually dawned on him that maybe it was right ***under his nose***, that is, what his family was doing for his grandmother.

3.  Most Home Instead clients have to pay ***out of*** their own ***pocket***, so that keeps the fees down.

4. Some of them are housewives who need to earn a couple of bucks just *to make ends meet*, you know.

5. In recent years, *scores of* other nonmedical home-care providers have been springing up.

**Explanation** > An idiom is a group of words with a special meaning that is different from the ordinary meaning of the separate words. There are countless idioms in American English. Below are some common idioms organized by three categories of meaning. The boldfaced idioms are from the report.

### Proximity/distance

*up the road*: within a short distance of walking or driving

*under [his] nose*: so close to someone that he or she should notice, but does not

*a stone's throw away*: very close

*in your face*: in a very direct and often shocking or surprising way

*too close for comfort*: not enough distance or privacy, making a person feel nervous or afraid

### Money

*out of pocket*: pay oneself, with no support

*make ends meet*: have just enough money to buy what you need

*be in the red*: owe more money than you have

*be in the black*: have money in your bank account; profitable

*cost an arm and a leg*: be very expensive

### Number/quantity

*scores of*: large amount of people or things

*a drop in the bucket*: an amount of something that is too small to have any effect

*dime a dozen*: very common, not valuable

*come up short*: not have enough of something when you need it, especially money

## Exercise

Read the following sentences.  Write the letter of the correct idiom to complete the sentences.

1. Many families cannot afford to send their older parents to a nursing home because it _____.

2. Although his insurance covered many of his medical expenses, he still had to pay for many of his medications _____.

3. When the agency realized that it was _____, it fired many of its employees.

4. When Hogan tried to find the money he needed to start his own company, he _____. So, he borrowed money.

5. Home-care agencies are a _____, but finding honest, well-trained caretakers to help care for an aging parent can be difficult.

6. It was easy for Hogan's grandmother to move in with his parents since they only lived _____.

7. Paul Hogan got _____ ideas for his new business from the cleaning franchise company he had worked for.

8. Many aging parents find the experience of living with their children's families _____, so they choose to live in nursing homes.

a. came up short

b. scores of

c. a stone's throw away

d. costs an arm and a leg

e. out of pocket

f. dime a dozen

g. in the red

h. too close for comfort

**B.    PRONUNCIATION: Thought Groups and Stress**

**Notice**    Listen to the excerpt from the report. Notice how the speaker groups words together. Notice also how one word or part of a word in each group has a higher pitch than the others. This word receives more stress.

My **grandmother** had **twelve** kids, **fifty-one** grandchildren,

**fifty great**-grandchildren by the time she **passed** away at **almost** 101.

**And** it seemed like it **took** every **one** of us to **keep** her

in the **home environment**. And the **question** in **my** mind and **Lori**,

my **wife**, I **mean**, what are **other** families **doing**?

**Explanation**    Speakers can help listeners follow their ideas by breaking up their sentences into thought groups. These act as verbal punctuation marks. They help listeners understand their meaning. Thought groups are often created with common phrases. For example, prepositional phrases are often divided into thought groups:

by the time she passed away . . .

at almost 101 . . .

Speakers also stress the more important words in each thought group. Notice how the boldfaced words in the above excerpt are pronounced with a higher pitch than the other words in the thought groups.

## Exercise 1

Listen to two more excerpts from the report. Underline the thought groups in each sentence. Circle the important words that have higher pitch.

1.    So back in 1994, when he was thirty-one, Hogan quit his job and he and his

wife Lori started Home Instead Senior Care to offer seniors a similar range of

services: cooking, cleaning, rides to church or the hairdresser. Within the first

year, they were profitable and the business has never stopped growing. Today

Home Instead has 425 franchises in the U.S. and dozens more abroad serving more than 25,000 elderly or disabled people.

2.  Roberta Ryan is getting buzzed into her client's apartment to bring her a bag of groceries.  Sixty-year-old Betty Ranigan has MS and had spinal surgery back in October, and it's been hard for her to do the things she did before.

### Exercise 2

Work in pairs.  Take turns reading the excerpts in Exercise 1.  Focus on the thought groups.  Use a higher pitch on the most important word.

## V.  FOLLOW-UP ACTIVITIES

### A.  DISCUSSION QUESTIONS

In groups, discuss your answers to the following questions.

1.  What is your reaction to the business Home Instead?  Do you think today's society needs this kind of service to care for elderly people?

2.  Some studies predict that by the year 2030, twenty percent of the world's population will be over the age of sixty-five.  What should we as a society do to prepare for this possibility?

3.  Having a job working with older or sick people can be very difficult, but it is also rewarding.  Would you like to have a job like this?  Why or why not?

### B.  DESIGN: A Quality Home-Care Service

1.  Take Notes to Prepare

By focusing on some of the details of the Home Instead business, you will be better able to complete the **design** activity that follows.

Listen to the report again.  Take notes on information about Home Instead.  Key phrases and some examples have been provided.

### Help needed by Hogan's grandmother

• *helping with meals* _____

_____

_____

_____

### Services provided by Home Instead

• *cooking* _____

_____

_____

_____

### Business operation

• *425 franchises in the United States* _____

_____

_____

_____

### Employees

• *$10/hour* _____

_____

_____

_____

## 2. Design

In the report, you heard about a new kind of home-care service. Home Instead was developed to help the elderly manage at home while providing some companionship. Work in groups. Design a quality home-care service. Your home-care service could help care for the elderly, the sick, or the disabled. Consider the criteria that you think would be necessary to become a licensed home-care service. Complete the following information about your service.

### Staff

Job requirements

_____

_____

_____

_____

_____

Work schedule

_____

_____

_____

_____

_____

Duties

_____

_____

_____

_____

_____

## Business Practices

Supervising staff

_____

_____

_____

Salaries

_____

_____

_____

Benefits/insurance

_____

_____

_____

Something unique about your service

_____

_____

_____

**"Home Instead" was first broadcast on _Weekend Edition_ on July 24, 2003. The reporter is Chris Arnold.**

# 10

# Living through Divorce

## I. ANTICIPATING THE ISSUES

### A. PREDICTING

Read the title and look at the photo. Discuss what you think the unit is about.

### B. THINKING AHEAD

In groups, discuss your answers to the following questions.

1. In the U.S. about half of marriages end in divorce. Is divorce a common problem in your country?

2. Who suffers more in a divorce, parents or children? Explain.

3. Should parents who get divorced explain the reasons to their children? Why or why not?

## II. ▶ VOCABULARY

Read the following sentences. The boldfaced words will help you understand the interview. Guess the meaning of these words from the context of the sentences. Then write a synonym or your own definition.

1. Children often feel alone and do not know who they can **turn to** when their parents get divorced.

   _____

2. For many children, **getting used to** living with one parent after a divorce is very difficult.

   _____

3. People often find it difficult to explain their reasons for divorce. Is it the parents' responsibility to **share** these reasons with their children?

   _____

4. When parents divorce, they should have **reassuring** conversations with their children to make them feel that everything will be all right.

   _____

5. A child's first dance or music **recital** is a big event. Children feel it is important for their parents to attend.

   _____

6. A good **guidance counselor** works with children in two ways: helping with school issues and giving advice about family problems.

   _____

7. Children suffer most when their parents first divorce; however, with time, they can usually **get through** it.

   _____

8.  It is very difficult for children to see one of their parents *packing up* to leave the home forever.

    _____

9.  When people divorce, it is usually not one person's *fault*. There have often been problems and difficulties with both people.

    _____

10. Authors sometimes decide to write a *series* of books if their first book has been successful.

    _____

**Match the words with their synonyms or definitions.**

_____  1.  turn to

_____  2.  get used to

_____  3.  share

_____  4.  reassuring

_____  5.  recital

_____  6.  guidance counselor

_____  7.  get through

_____  8.  pack up

_____  9.  fault

_____ 10.  series

a.  performance of a piece of music, dance, etc.

b.  ask for help, advice, or sympathy

c.  responsibility for something bad

d.  someone who works in a school giving advice to students

e.  put things in bags to take them somewhere

f.  manage to deal with a difficult situation

g.  tell someone about an idea, secret, problem, etc.

h.  become more comfortable with a situation

i.  making someone feel less worried

j.  a group of books or events that happen one after another

## III. LISTENING

### A. TASK LISTENING

Listen to the interview. Find the answer to the following question.

Why is Betsy concerned about divorce?

### B. LISTENING FOR MAIN IDEAS

Read the questions for each part. Listen to the interview again. It is divided into three parts. You will hear a beep at the end of each part. As you listen, circle the answer that expresses the main idea in that part. Compare your answers with those of a partner.

**Part 1**  Why did Betsy Allison Walter write to the mayor about her parents' divorce?

    a. She thought he was responsible for divorces in New York.

    b. She thought he was a good parent and would understand.

    c. She thought he knew a lot of things.

**Part 2**  How does Betsy feel about the advice that is given to her?

    a. She realizes that she is the only child with her problem.

    b. She still does not understand why her parents are getting divorced.

    c. She now understands why her parents can't stay together.

**Part 3**  What advice does Betsy give other children in her book?

    a. She tells them that it is their fault if their parents get divorced.

    b. She tells them not to cry.

    c. She says they should tell someone about their feelings.

## C.  LISTENING FOR DETAILS

Read the statements for Part 1.  Then listen to Part 1 again and decide whether the statements are true or false.  As you listen, write *T* or *F* next to each statement. Compare your answers with those of a partner.  If you disagree, listen again.

### Part 1

_____  1.  Betsy Allison Walter is nine years old.

_____  2.  Betsy lives in Manhattan.

_____  3.  Betsy knew who to turn to.

_____  4.  Betsy's father is with somebody else.

_____  5.  Mayor Koch wrote back to Betsy.

_____  6.  Mayor Koch gave her a solution to her problem.

_____  7.  His letter was reassuring to Betsy.

_____  8.  Betsy had hoped that the mayor would call her father.

_____  9.  Betsy's parents sat next to each other at her dance recital.

Repeat the same procedure for Parts 2 and 3.

### Part 2

_____  10.  Four hundred kids in Betsy's school have the same problem.

_____  11.  The interviewer says most people have parents who are divorced.

_____  12.  *The Boys' and Girls' Book of Divorce* was written by a psychologist.

_____  13.  Betsy went out to buy his other book.

_____  14.  She loved his book.

_____  15.  Betsy feels satisfied with people's answers about divorce.

_____  16.  She thinks parents sometimes hide their reasons for divorce.

_____  17.  Her father left the house.

_____  18.  Betsy wants her parents to get divorced.

> **Part 3**

_____ 19. Betsy wrote a short book.

_____ 20. She reads the whole book in the interview.

_____ 21. The interviewer gives Betsy advice about her parents.

_____ 22. Betsy wants to be a writer and write a series of books.

_____ 23. She would like to be rich.

_____ 24. She would like to be famous.

**D.   LISTENING FOR INFERENCE**

Read the following questions.  Then listen to the excerpts from the interview.  Focus on the interviewer's response to Betsy.  Answer the questions.  Compare your answers with those of a partner.  Listen again if necessary.

**Excerpt 1**

1.  How does the interviewer respond to Betsy?

   _____

2.  Why do you think he responds this way?

   _____

3.  Do you think Betsy is satisfied with his response?

   _____

**Excerpt 2**

4.  How does the interviewer respond to Betsy?

   _____

5.  Why do you think he responds this way?

   _____

6.  Do you think Betsy is satisfied with his response?

   _____

# IV. LOOKING AT LANGUAGE

## A. USAGE: Wishes

**Notice**

Listen to the excerpt from the interview. Focus on the boldfaced words. Why does Betsy change the verb? Is her verb change correct?

> Thank you for the letter. I was saddened to learn of the difficult times you are experiencing now. It is important for you to share your feelings and thoughts with someone during this time. I ***wish there is . . . was*** an easy solution to these problems, but there is not. Please remember that you are loved and the pe—. . . that people care about you.
>
> All the best.
>
> Sincerely,
>
> Edward Koch

**Explanation**

People often make mistakes when using *wish* statements. In the excerpt, Betsy uses the present tense (*is*) while reading the letter. Then she corrects herself and reads the past tense (*was*) that is written. This use of *was* is sometimes used in informal speech. However, the correct statement is: *I wish there **were** an easy solution . . .* [Note: *Were* is used for both singular and plural subjects.]

We use *wish* statements when we want reality to be different (or the opposite). If the reality is affirmative, the wish statement is negative. If the reality is negative, the wish statement is affirmative. *Wish* is followed by a noun clause and can refer to wishes about the future, present, or past. The verb tenses change to past forms in the noun clause following *wish*.

|  | REALITY | WISH |
|---|---|---|
| Wish about the future | Future tense (*will*) | Past form of *will* (*would*) |
|  | Betsy's parents **will get** divorced. | Betsy wishes her parents **wouldn't get** divorced. |
| Wish about the present | Present tense | Past tense |
|  | Betsy **doesn't know** why her parents are getting a divorce. | Betsy wishes she **knew** why her parents are getting a divorce. |
| Wish about the past | Past tense | Past perfect |
|  | Betsy's parents **didn't sit** together at her recital. | Betsy wishes her parents **had sat** together at her recital. |

## Exercise

Complete the following sentences with the correct form of the verb.

1. Betsy doesn't know who to turn to. She wishes she _____ who to turn to.

2. Betsy's father left to be with someone else. She wishes he _____ to be with someone else.

3. Mayor Koch's letter was not reassuring to Betsy. She wishes Mayor Koch's letter _____ more reassuring.

4. People will tell Betsy the same thing over and over. Betsy wishes they _____ her the same thing over and over.

5. Parents will sometimes hide some information from children. Betsy wishes they _____ so much information from children.

6. Betsy saw her father packing up to leave. He probably wishes she _____ him packing up to leave.

7. No one can advise Betsy well.  Betsy wishes someone

   _____ her well.

8. Children won't always tell people how they feel about their parents' divorce.

   Betsy wishes they _____ people how they feel.

## B.   PRONUNCATION: Intonation for Questions

**Notice**

Listen to the excerpt from the interview.  Focus on the intonation patterns of the three questions.  Does the intonation rise or fall in each of the three questions?

ADAMS:   Can you give me an example, Betsy?

BETSY:     Why did they get divorced? What happened?

**Explanation**

The first question is a *Yes/No* question.  These questions usually end with a rising intonation.  In the excerpt, the *Yes/No* question was answered with two *wh*-questions.  *Wh-* questions usually end with a falling intonation.

Sometimes a question has a statement pattern.  These types of questions can end with either a rising or falling intonation pattern.

### Exercise 1

Listen to the questions from the interview.  Determine each question's intonation pattern.  Circle *rising* or *falling*.

1. And you're eight years old?                          rising        falling

2. And you live in Manhattan?                           rising        falling

3. Why did you write to . . . to Mayor Koch?            rising        falling

4. Did you get an answer back?                          rising        falling

5. What'd he say?                                       rising        falling

6. Was that reassuring to you, in a way?               rising        falling

| | | |
|---|---|---|
| 7. No? | rising | falling |
| 8. What other advice have you been able to come across? To . . . to find? | rising | falling |
| 9. You wrote another letter to somebody who, who had written a book called *The Boys' and Girls' Book of Divorce*? | rising | falling |
| 10. A psychologist? | rising | falling |
| 11. And what did that person tell you? | rising | falling |
| 12. Did you? | rising | falling |
| 13. And how did that go? | rising | falling |
| 14. What did you think of that one? | rising | falling |
| 15. And in terms of their own divorce, do you understand it better now? | rising | falling |
| 16. No? | rising | falling |
| 17. Why did they have to go off and do it? | rising | falling |
| 18. You wrote a very small book? | rising | falling |
| 19. Do you have it there? | rising | falling |
| 20. Could you read some of it for me, please? | rising | falling |
| 21. Why does it have to be you? | rising | falling |

## Exercise 2

Work in pairs.  Take turns reading the questions above.  Focus on the intonation patterns.

# V. FOLLOW-UP ACTIVITIES

## A. DISCUSSION QUESTIONS

In groups, discuss your answers to the following questions.

1. Betsy wanted her parents to sit together during her dance recital, but they did not. In your opinion, do divorced parents have an obligation to be together at important times in their child's life? How can families best deal with this issue?

2. In Betsy's school, 75 percent of the children have parents who are divorced (300 out of 400). This percentage is not unusual in the United States. How does this percentage differ from the divorce rate in your country? What are the reasons for the difference or similarity?

3. Betsy's parents did not explain to her their reasons for getting divorced. If you were Betsy's parents, would you discuss the reasons with her? Does it help children to accept their parents' divorce if they know the reasons for it?

## B. CASE STUDIES: The Question of Divorce

### 1. Take Notes to Prepare

By focusing on Betsy's experience with divorce in her family, you will be better able to discuss the **case studies** that follow.

Listen to the interview again. Take notes on Betsy's story. Key phrases and some examples have been provided.

Advice given to Betsy

• It's important to share feelings. _____

_____

_____

_____

Persons giving advice to Betsy

• The mayor of New York

_____

_____

_____

_____

Betsy's questions and feelings about divorce

• Who should she turn to?

_____

_____

_____

_____

Betsy's advice to others about divorce

• It's not your fault.

_____

_____

_____

_____

✓ **2.  Case Studies**

You have listened to a young girl express her feelings about her parents' divorce. You most likely have your own opinions on this issue.

Work in groups.  Read each case.  Then act as a group of family counselors. Discuss each case and agree on advice for each person.  Take notes on your group's discussion.  You can use the chart on page 29 as a model for organizing your notes.  Then compare suggestions with other groups.

**Case 1: Betsy (age 8)**

"My parents are getting divorced, and I really don't know who to turn to.  My dad met another woman.  I was just getting used to my life, and now this!  It's really kind of hard on me.  I invited both my parents to my dance recital, but they didn't sit next to each other.  It was painful to see my dad packing up to leave. They won't explain anything to me."

### Case 2: George (age 66)

"My son has been married for ten years. His wife is a wonderful young woman. Over the years, my wife and I have grown quite attached to her. In fact, she's like a daughter to us. We've spent all the family holidays with them and we have even gone on vacations with them. Now, after ten years, my son has decided to go off with another woman. He is divorcing his wife so that he can be with this new woman. We are very fond of our daughter-in-law but don't know whether or not we should continue our relationship with her. Our son doesn't want us to continue seeing her."

### Case 3: Carolyn (age 28)

"I married my husband five years ago. I was twenty-three years old . . . too young to know what I was doing. My life with him has become very boring. We never go out. We don't have any friends. I no longer want to be with him because we don't have anything in common. We have a two-year-old daughter, and I haven't wanted to think about getting a divorce. But I'm afraid that if my husband and I stay together, it will be even worse for her."

### Case 4: John (age 44)

"I have been dating a married woman for six months now. She's been in a very unhappy marriage for years and is going to be getting a divorce soon. We've fallen In love and want to spend as much time together as possible. The problem is her son. Every time I go over to her house, I feel guilty because of her child. I know that he misses his father and doesn't appreciate me visiting his mother at the house. It's difficult for our relationship because we can't easily get together without her son. I don't know if I should continue this relationship until the divorce is final. In fact, I don't know if the relationship will ever work out because of her child and his relationship to his father."

### Case 5: Joyce (age 50)

"I have been happily married for thirty years. This year my husband started acting differently toward me. He didn't seem to be interested in doing anything with me anymore. Finally I realized what had happened. He was seeing another woman. This other woman is half my age. She's twenty-five! I'm so depressed. I never thought that this could happen to me. My husband and I have discussed the matter; we've decided to get a divorce. My children are grown up and living on their own. I don't want to tell them about their father because I'm too ashamed."

**"Living through Divorce"** was first broadcast on *All Things Considered*, **February 11, 1987. The interviewer is Noah Adams.**

# 11

# Meet You on the Air

### A. PREDICTING

Read the title and look at the photo. Discuss what you think the unit is about.

### B. THINKING AHEAD

In groups, discuss your answers to the following questions.

1. What do you like to do on Saturday nights? Do you think it is important to go out? Why or why not?

2. Some people think it is difficult to find someone to go on a date. How do people meet in your country?

3. Some Americans write personal ads to meet people. Here is an example:

> Single, attractive, professional female seeks handsome professional man (25–30 yrs.) who likes his work and loves to dance.

These people hope that someone will read their ad in a newspaper, magazine, or online and be interested in meeting them. What do you think of this method of meeting people?

## II. VOCABULARY

The words in the first column will help you understand the interview. Try to guess their meaning. Then read each set of words. Cross out the word that does not have a similar meaning to the word in the first column. Use a dictionary if you need help. Compare your answers with those of a partner. Discuss why these words are similar.

1. **date**          person to go          girlfriend/boyfriend          ~~place~~
                     out with

2. **singles**          unmarried people          married people          people who
                                                                          are alone

3. **chat**          have a long          engage in small talk          have a short
                     discussion                                          conversation

4. **match-maker**          person who          go-between          wife
                            arranges marriages

5. **promoted**          helped          destroyed          advertised

6. **banter**          playful talking          joking          arguing

7. **sizzling**          unusual          burning          passionate

8. **eccentric**          unusual person          strange person          friendly person

9. **bland**          mild          uninteresting          old

## III. LISTENING

### A. TASK LISTENING

Listen to the interview. You will hear different people talking. As you listen, check (✓) the subjects the people talk about.

_____ playing the piano          _____ looking for a job

_____ reading books          _____ eating Chinese food

_____ going to the beach          _____ drinking

## B.    LISTENING FOR MAIN IDEAS

Read the questions for each part. Listen to the interview again. It is divided into four parts. You will hear a beep at the end of each part. As you listen, circle the answer that expresses the main idea in that part. Compare your answers with those of a partner.

**Part 1**    What is *Date Night*?

a.  a radio show for singles

b.  a new club for singles

c.  a music show on the radio

**Part 2**    How did *Date Night* get started?

a.  Susan Block needed information to write a book.

b.  Susan Block wanted to match up people on the air.

c.  Radio listeners asked Susan Block to start it.

**Part 3**    How would you describe the conversations on the show?

a.  light conversations

b.  serious conversations

c.  debates about important topics

**Part 4**    According to Susan Block, why are the personal ads on this show better than personal ads in the paper?

a.  They are edited more carefully.

b.  They are more bland than the personals in the paper.

c.  They give you a sense of the person's personality through their voice.

## C.    LISTENING FOR DETAILS

Read the questions for Part 1. Then listen to Part 1 again. As you listen, circle the best answers. Compare your answers with those of a partner. If you disagree, listen again.

### Part 1

1.  Which of the following is *not* true about *Date Night*?

    a.  It's a call-in show.

    b.  It's in Los Angeles.

    c.  It's a radio station.

2.  What do people do after they meet on the air?

    a.  They meet in Los Angeles.

    b.  They write to each other's box number.

    c.  They become matchmakers.

3.  Who is John?

    a.  a matchmaker

    b.  a famous musician

    c.  someone looking for a date

4.  Who is Linda?

    a.  the host of *Date Night*

    b.  C.J.'s friend

    c.  a woman whom John wants to talk to

Repeat the same procedure for Parts 2–4.

### Part 2

5.  What did the show's host do?

    a.  She wrote a book on how to play the personals.

    b.  She wrote personal ads about herself.

    c.  She called people who wrote personal ads.

6. What did Susan Block do on her talk show before *Date Night* started?

    a. She would make up personal ads for people.

    b. She expressed her feelings about dating on the air.

    c. She matched up single people who needed each other.

## Part 3

7. What is the banter on the show like?

    a. like banter in a singles' bar

    b. like banter at work

    c. like banter in the movies

8. Which kind of Chinese food is *not* talked about?

    a. sizzling chicken

    b. hot and sour soup

    c. stuffed dumplings

9. What does the man say you must do when you eat Chinese food?

    a. take off your shoes

    b. share your plates

    c. use chopsticks

## Part 4

10. What are personal ads on *Date Night*?

    a. fifteen-word messages

    b. newspaper personals

    c. audio personals

11. According to Susan Block, which are the *best* personals?

    a. the ones with the most information

    b. the ones with nice personalities

    c. the ones with music in the background

12. What does Robert say about himself?

    a. He's thirty-three years old.

    b. He's a passionate eccentric.

    c. He finds women very beautiful.

13. Why doesn't Susan Block like the ads in the paper?

    a. They are too bland.

    b. The information is not true.

    c. The people do not sound attractive.

14. What does she tell people to do when they call in to put ads on her show?

    a. be themselves

    b. be bland

    c. be outrageous

15. What does the woman who calls in say about herself?

    a. She embarrassed somebody she went out with.

    b. She is looking for somebody that is looking for somebody.

    c. Her name is Amy.

## D. LISTENING FOR INFERENCE

This interview includes two personal ads. Read the following questions. Then listen to the excerpts from the interview. Circle three adjectives that best describe the personality of the person in the ad. Compare your answers with those of a partner. Listen again if necessary.

### Excerpt 1

1. Which adjectives best describe Robert?

    self-centered      sad        shy

    funny              strong     dishonest

**Excerpt 2**

2. Which adjectives best describe Annie?

lonely     fun     proud

bland     eccentric     insecure

# IV. LOOKING AT LANGUAGE

## A. USAGE: Two-Word Verbs

**Notice**

Listen to the excerpts from the interview. Focus on the boldfaced words. Guess their meaning from context. Discuss your ideas with a partner.

1. I had a wonderful night tonight, I **had** guests **over**, played the piano, had a lot of fun, oh, great.

2. And sometimes what I'd do with a call-in show is, somebody would call in, and—say it was Linda—and I would **make up** a personal for Linda.

3. And she would express herself and then **get off** the air.

4. And then maybe Bob would **call in** and say, 'Hey, that Linda, she sounded great, how can I meet her?'

5. And I would just feel terrible that I couldn't **match up** poor Bob and poor Linda, who were two single people who needed each other. And I thought, 'I'm gonna do a show like this myself. I'm gonna **match** people **up** on the air,' and that's how *Date Night* started.

6. **Tune in** next week; same time, same station, for another Saturday night on *Date Night*.

**Explanation**

Many verbs in English are made up of two words: a verb + a particle. When these two words are combined, they usually have a new meaning.

Some two-word verbs are separable. This means that the verb and particle can be separated by an object.

I'm gonna **match** people **up** on the air.

The object can go between the verb and particle, or after the verb and particle.

I'm gonna **match up** people.

However, if the direct object is a pronoun, it *must* go between the verb and particle.

I'm gonna **match** them **up**.

## Exercise

Read the following sentences. Each two-word verb is separable. Rewrite the sentences using pronouns as direct objects.

1. Some people don't want to **give up** their freedom just to have a steady boyfriend or girlfriend.

   Some people don't want to give it up just to have a steady boyfriend

   or girlfriend.

2. In the United States, many people go out in cars. It is common for a man to **pick up** his date at her home.

   _____

   _____

3. People who are engaged to be married sometimes **call off** their engagement just before the wedding.

   _____

   _____

4. Some women would like to ask men out for a date, but it's hard for them to pick up the phone and **call up** men.

   _____

   _____

5. Some women will go out with a man they've never met before; but it's better to **check out** a man before going on the first date.

   _____

   _____

**B.**   **PRONUNCIATION: Two-Word Verbs**

**Notice**   Listen to the excerpts from the interview.  Focus on the boldfaced words. Which word is stressed: the verb (the first word) or the particle (the second word)?

1. And she would express herself and then ***get off*** the air.

2. And I would just feel terrible that I couldn't ***match up*** poor Bob and poor Linda, who were two single people who needed each other.  And I thought, 'I'm gonna do a show like this myself.  I'm gonna ***match*** people ***up*** on the air, and that's how *Date Night* started.'

3. ***Tune in*** next week; same time, same station, for another Saturday night on *Date Night*.

**Explanation**   In two-word verbs, both the verb and the particle can be stressed.  In the above examples, the particles are stressed in the two-word verbs.  The particle may have more stress when a particle ends a sentence or when a pronoun separates the verb and particle.

I'm gonna match people **up´**.

I'm gonna match them **up´** on the air.

### Exercise 1

Complete the following dialogues with the correct two-word verbs.  Separate the verbs and particles with pronouns.

|          |          |          |
|----------|----------|----------|
| call off | have over | put off  |
| call up  | make up  | turn off |
| give up  | match up |          |

1. A: Hey, how are the plans for your wedding going?

   B: Terrible. In fact, I'm about ready to _____.

2. A: Are you still dating?

   B: Well, I was about to _____ until I heard about *Date Night*.

3. A: Don't you think Joseph and Sarah would get along well?

   B: Yes, that's a great idea!  Why don't we _____?

4. A: Have you seen that girl that you talked to on *Date Night* yet?

   B: Not yet, but I was thinking I might _____ to my house this weekend.

5. A: I love the way that guy sounds on *Date Night*!

   B: Really? Well, why don't you _____ then? Here's the phone.

6. A: You were supposed to have a date with Eva last night, weren't you?

   B: I know, but we _____ until next week.

7. A: Do you want to keep listening to the radio?

   B: No, I'm tired. Let's _____.

8. A: Do you believe the things people write in their personal ads?

   B: I don't know. I think a lot of people just _____.

## Exercise 2

Work in pairs. Take turns reading the dialogues above. Focus on stressing the particles in the two-word verbs.

# V. FOLLOW-UP ACTIVITIES

## A. DISCUSSION QUESTIONS

In groups, discuss your answers to the following questions.

1. Would you call in to a radio show like *Date Night* to meet somebody? Why or why not?

2. Susan Block said that some typical questions asked on *Date Night* were: "What kind of work do you do?;" "What movies have you seen?;" and "Do you like Chinese food?" What questions would you ask a person when you first meet? What questions would you *not* ask a person when you first meet?

3. Today people often talk about how difficult it is to meet someone. Do you think that it is more difficult than it was in the past? Why or why not?

## B. VALUES CLARIFICATION: Dating

### 1. Take Notes to Prepare

By focusing on what people talk about and how they present themselves in the interview, you will be better able to complete the **values clarification** activity that follows.

Listen to the interview again. Take notes on how the callers looking for a date describe themselves. What categories of information are included in their descriptions? Some examples have been provided.

Characteristics of people looking for a date:

<u>Social</u>_____     _____

<u>Musical</u>_____     _____

_____     _____

_____     _____

_____     _____

_____     _____

_____     _____

_____     _____

### 2. Values Clarification

Work in groups. Discuss what you look for in a person and why. Read the list of qualities that people typically want to find in a date.

Each person in the group ranks the qualities from 1 (most important) to 6 (least important). What other qualities would you include? Add them to the list. Share your rankings with your group. Try to agree on one group ranking.

_____ **Education**

The person should be well educated. He or she should be intelligent. The person should have gone to good schools and should have a broad understanding of the world.

_____     **Good looks**

The person should be attractive.  Dress and appearance are very important.

_____     **Humor**

The person should know how to laugh at life.  Being able to joke about things is important.

_____     **Personality**

The person should be very social and be able to get along with many different types of people.  He or she should like to go to parties and meet new people.

_____     **Wealth**

The person should have a lot of money.  Money is important in today's world, so it is important to be with someone who can afford to pay for nice things, go on trips, and so on.

**Other:** _____

"Meet You on the Air" was first broadcast on *All Things Considered*, April 16, 1986. The interviewer is Wendy Kaufman.

# 12

# Running on Vegetable Oil?

## I. ANTICIPATING THE ISSUE

### A. PREDICTING

Read the title and look at the photo. Discuss what you think the unit is about.

### B. THINKING AHEAD

In groups, discuss your answers to the following questions.

1. What is your biggest concern regarding the environment? Why?

2. In your opinion, what is the greatest energy problem we face today? What can individuals do about it? What can governments do?

## II. ▸ VOCABULARY

Read the following sentences. The boldfaced words will help you understand the interview. Guess the meaning of these words from the context of the sentences. Then write a synonym or your own definition.

1. One of the biggest challenges for our future will be finding and developing **alternative** sources of energy.

   _____

2. Because the scientist **synthesizes** these new drugs, they can be sold more cheaply.

   _____

3. Since chain stores, like Starbucks and Benneton, have become popular, many **mom-and-pop** stores have disappeared.

   _____

4. Sophia likes expensive things, so she only shops in **high-end** stores.

   _____

5. When I told my boss I was quitting my job, he just gave me a **blank stare**.

   _____

6. My mother often got **cravings** for ice cream late at night, just before she went to bed.

   _____

7. Last year the city lost 5,000 jobs and added 15,000 different jobs. The **net gain** was 10,000 jobs.

   _____

8. Because I love gardening, my favorite topic in Biology was **photosynthesis**.

   _____

9. We can save money buying food if we join our local food **co-ops**.

_____

10. Many people who live in the area are **Greens**. This year, they have been working to protect the wetlands and clean up the beach areas.

_____

11. The hurricane was terrible, but it was also **unifying**. The whole town worked together to rebuild the community.

_____

12. Maybe we cannot agree on every political issue, but when we discuss the future of our children, we should be able to establish some **common ground**.

_____

Match the words with their synonyms or definitions.

_____  1. alternative

_____  2. synthesize

_____  3. mom-and-pop

_____  4. high-end

_____  5. blank stare

_____  6. craving

_____  7. net gain

_____  8. photosynthesis

_____  9. co-op

_____ 10. Green

_____ 11. unifying

_____ 12. common ground

a. a look showing no expression or understanding

b. combine different things in order to produce something

c. what remains after things have been added and taken away

d. different from what is usual or accepted

e. bringing people together

f. expensive; of good quality

g. person who works politically to protect the environment

h. very strong desire for something

i. a company, farm, etc. that is owned and operated by people working together

j. facts, opinions, and beliefs that people can agree on, in a situation in which they are arguing about something

k. the way that green plants make their food using the light from the sun

l. independent; family-owned

# III. LISTENING

## A. TASK LISTENING

Listen to the interview.  Find the answer to the following question.

To run on biodiesel, what kind of changes must be made to cars?

## B. LISTENING FOR MAIN IDEAS

Read the questions for each part.  Listen to the interview again. It is divided into four parts.  You will hear a beep at the end of each part.  As you listen, circle the answer that expresses the main idea in that part.  Compare your answers with those of a partner.

**Part 1**    What did Mike Pelly do?

    a.  He became a famous chemist.

    b.  He created his own biodiesel.

    c.  He developed a new vegetable oil.

**Part 2**    Where is the best place for Mike to get oil?

    a.  in Chinese restaurants

    b.  from farmers

    c.  at McDonald's

**Part 3**    Why is his system better for the environment?

    a.  It has a better smell.

    b.  It stops global warming.

    c.  It pulls $CO_2$ out of the atmosphere.

| Part 4 | What is Mike Pelly marketing? |

    a. biodiesel

    b. machinery

    c. new fuel-efficient cars

## C. LISTENING FOR DETAILS

Read the statements for Part 1. Then listen to Part 1 again and decide whether the statements are true or false. As you listen, write *T* or *F* next to each statement. Compare your answers with those of a partner. If you disagree, listen again.

| Part 1 |

_____ 1. This country (the United States) is not dependent on foreign sources of oil.

_____ 2. Mike Pelly has been working on biodiesel for ten years.

_____ 3. Pelly made his biodiesel in a chemistry lab.

_____ 4. Pelly makes his biodiesel from vegetable oil.

Repeat the same procedure for Parts 2–4.

| Part 2 |

_____ 5. Pelly runs his car 100 percent on vegetables.

_____ 6. Pelly gets his vegetable oil from his mom and pop.

_____ 7. Asian restaurant oil is better quality than other restaurant oil.

_____ 8. Farmers can grow the oil for biodiesel.

_____ 9. Folks are surprised that he wants the oil that they throw out.

_____ 10. Pelly pays people to pick up their oil.

_____ 11. His car smells like food.

> **Part 3**

_____ 12. Using biodiesel is cleaner for the car's engine.

_____ 13. Biodiesel helps the problem of global warming.

_____ 14. Growing vegetables takes $CO_2$ out of the atmosphere.

_____ 15. Growing vegetables takes out more $CO_2$ from the atmosphere than a car tailpipe puts into it.

> **Part 4**

_____ 16. Pelly makes money by selling fuel.

_____ 17. Pelly already sells machinery to farm co-ops and urban fuel co-ops.

_____ 18. Trucking companies are tired of paying so much for fuel.

_____ 19. The Pacific Northwest has been a big user of biodiesel for five years.

_____ 20. Biodiesel unifies Greens and Republican farmers.

_____ 21. Pelly's company is called "Olympia Green Use."

_____ 22. The price of his fuel is $1.14 a gallon.

## D. LISTENING FOR INFERENCE

Read the following statements. Then listen to the excerpts from the interview. Decide whether you agree or disagree with the statements, based on the attitudes of the speakers. Circle your answers. Compare your answers with those of a partner. Listen again if necessary.

### Excerpt 1

1. Mr. Pelly gets cravings to stop and eat when he drives his car.                    Agree    Disagree

2. People driving behind Mr. Pelly's cars get cravings to stop and eat.               Agree    Disagree

**Excerpt 2**

3. Mr. Pelly is a Republican. Agree Disagree

4. Mr. Pelly thinks people are usually Agree Disagree
too divided on issues.

# IV. LOOKING AT LANGUAGE

## A. USAGE: Hyphenated Adjectives

**Notice**

Listen to the excerpts from the interview. Focus on the underlined words. How do they function in the sentences? Why are they written with hyphens?

1. For the past decade, the carpenter-turned-backyard chemist has fueled his two cars with homemade biodiesel which he synthesizes from used vegetable oil; that's what we're told.

2. We like to go to various restaurants, usually mom-and-pop restaurants, high-end restaurants, and, for some reason, Asian restaurants, a lot of places that throw out their oil a little sooner than others.

**Explanation**

The underlined phrases function as adjectives. We use a hyphen for most compound adjectives that precede a noun. Following are some general rules about hyphenated adjectives.

1. Compound adjectives formed with an adjective and a noun with a -d or -ed ending are always hyphenated:

an old-fashioned system of transportation

a multi-layered engine

2. Compound adjectives formed with a noun, adjective, or adverb and a present participle are always hyphenated:

an oil-producing country

strong-smelling emissions

Note: If the adverb ends in *-ly* in an adverb-adjective compound, do *not* use a hyphen:

> a finely tuned machine

> cheaply priced gasoline

3. Compound adjectives formed with numbers and measurements are usually hyphenated:

> a ten-year-old experiment

> a twelve-inch tailpipe

4. Compound adjectives formed with *high-* or *low-* are generally hyphenated:

> high-end restaurants

> low-budget biodiesel

5. Compound adjectives formed with adverbs such as *well-*, *best-*, and *least-* and an adjective or participle are hyphenated:

> well-known scientist

> best-loved car

> least-favorite idea

6. Hyphenated adjectives are usually descriptive and give a literary element to a sentence:

> a carpenter-turned-backyard chemist

> a new, save-the-earth fuel

## Exercise

Write the following expressions with hyphenated adjectives.  Use the rules above to help you.

1. a car with three wheels = _____

2. an idea that will provoke our thoughts = _____

3. a family that has two cars = _____

4. a restaurant that is run by a family = _____

5. a reaction that is extremely excited = _____

6. food that is deep fried = _____

7. a restaurant that serves fast food = _____

8. emissions that produce $CO_2$ = _____

9. machinery that makes biodiesel = _____

10. an engine that is well built = _____

11. a topic that is widely discussed = _____

12. a bill for clean energy = _____

## B.   PRONUNCIATION: Dropped Syllables

**Notice**   Read the excerpts from the interview. How many syllables are there in each boldfaced word?

1. Where do you get the ***vegetable*** oil?

2. We like to go to various ***restaurants***, ***usually*** mom-and-pop restaurants, high-end restaurants, and, for some reason, Asian restaurants, a lot of places that throw their oil out a little sooner than others.

3. It's the first fuel where you ***actually*** did not have to do anything to an already-built car.

4. And from there, we can talk about other things ***comfortably***.

Now listen to the excerpts. How many syllables do you hear pronounced in each boldfaced word?

**Explanation**   In many English words, unstressed syllables are sometimes dropped. In each of the underlined words in the excerpts above, there is one less pronounced syllable than its written form. If you look these words up in the dictionary, you will find them separated into more syllables.

| SYLLABLES IN WRITTEN FORM | SYLLABLES IN SPOKEN FORM |
|---|---|
| veg-e-ta-ble | vɛdʒ-tə-bəl |
| res-tau-rants | res-trənt |
| u-sual-ly | yuʒ-li |
| ac-tu-al-ly | ɛk-tʃə-li |
| com-for-tab-ly | kam-ftə-bli |

## Exercise 1

Listen to the following sentences.  Each underlined word has a dropped syllable.
Cross out the dropped syllable.

1. With the <u>usual</u> energy shortages, there should be a big <u>interest</u> in biodiesel in the near future.

2. Biodiesel is <u>generally</u> more popular with people living in the Northwest than it is for the <u>average</u> person living in other parts of the U.S.

3. In the future, people will look for new ways to keep their homes heated at <u>comfortable</u> <u>temperatures</u>.

4. Mike Pelly's <u>favorite</u> places to pick up used oil are Chinese <u>restaurants</u>.

5. These places throw out their <u>vegetable</u> oil <u>practically</u> every time they finish cooking with it.

6. When Pelly burns oil to run his car, it produces <u>different</u>, <u>separate</u> smells of either Chinese food, barbecued chicken, or potato chips.

## Exercise 2

Work in pairs.  Take turns reading the sentences.  Remember that some syllables are dropped.

# V. FOLLOW-UP ACTIVITIES

## A. DISCUSSION QUESTIONS

In groups, discuss your answers to these questions.

1. Do you think most cars will be running on vegetable oil in the near future? Why or why not?

2. What do you think the "Green" position regarding energy is? What do you think the "Republican farmers" position regarding energy is? Why might they be different?

3. People who use vegetable oil for fuel also help out the people who need to get rid of their vegetable oil. Can you think of another product that people generally throw away that could be a help to someone else? Explain.

## B. SURVEY: Energy Solutions

### 1. Take Notes to Prepare

By focusing on some ideas in the development of biodiesel, you will better be able to prepare questions for the **survey** that follows.

Listen to the interview again. Take notes on biodiesel information. Key phrases and some examples have been provided.

Problems

• This country is dependent on foreign oil.

_____

_____

_____

_____

Advantages of Biodiesel solution

• Uses vegetable oil thrown out by restaurants.

_____

_____

_____

Potential users

• Farm co-ops.

_____

_____

_____

Political implications

• Unifies two opposite political views.

_____

_____

_____

## ✓ 2. Survey

Work in groups. Write a survey questionnaire. Write five *Yes/No* questions that ask people's opinions about our energy problems. For example, you can ask about running cars and trucks, heating and cooling buildings, or understanding political concerns. Decide where and when you will conduct the survey, how many people you will question, who they will be, and so on.

Conduct your survey. Count the *yes* and *no* responses and take notes on people's comments. You can use the following chart to write your questions, count responses, and record comments.

| Questions | Yes | No | Comments |
|---|---|---|---|
| Example: *Do you think all cars will ever be run on an alternative fuel like biodiesel?* | Ⅲℍ // | // | *Yes. We will surely run out of fossil fuels soon. We will have to find an alternative solution.* *No. People are not ready to change their behaviors.* |
| 1. | | | |
| 2. | | | |
| 3. | | | |
| 4. | | | |
| 5. | | | |

**Oral Report**

When your group meets again, summarize the information you have collected from each question. Prepare an oral report to present to the class. Be sure to include an introduction to your survey, a summary of the results, and a conclusion. The conclusion should include your own interpretation of the information you collected.

**Oral Presentation Procedures**

1. The first student introduces the group and gives an introduction to the survey that was conducted.

2. The next few students present one or two of the questions that were asked, statistics or general responses that were received, and comments that were made by the people who were interviewed. The comments mentioned should help explain why people answered the way they did.

3. The last student concludes the presentation by summarizing the information from the survey, interpreting it, and perhaps reacting to the results. (For example, "We were surprised to learn that most people thought . . .")

**Useful Words and Phrases**

When you talk about the people who answered your survey, you can call them:

- interviewees

- respondents

When you report the information you gathered, you can begin:

- They agreed that . . .

- They stated that . . .

- They felt that . . .

- They believed that . . .

When you indicate the number of people surveyed, you can say:

- More than half agreed that . . .

- Almost three-quarters said that . . .

- Less than a third said that . . .

- More than 50 percent of the sample stated that . . .

"Running on Vegetable Oil?" was first broadcast on *All Things Considered*, June 29, 2005.  The interviewer is Steve Inskeep.